The Good Widow

A MEMOIR OF LIVING WITH LOSS

JENNIFER KATZ

SHE WRITES PRESS

Published 2021
Printed in the United States of America
Print ISBN: 978-1-64742-149-6
E-ISBN: 978-1-64742-150-2
Library of Congress Control Number: 2021904335

For information, address:
She Writes Press
1569 Solano Ave #546
Berkeley, CA 94707

She Writes Press is a division of SparkPoint Studio, LLC.

For Tristram, Jonah, and Maddy—
my loves, my forever family

Contents

PART III: HALTING STEPS FORWARD

PREFACE

G rief is unforgiving.

At times, grief ambushes the bereaved—pulling us back into the past. At other times, we willingly go back in time to connect with memories of those we've lost. We gaze at old photos, murmuring appreciation for the bright smiles they preserve. We talk about our loved ones, reliving the milestones, telling stories of holidays and happiness, of hospitals and horror. Along with pain and despair, we feel gratitude for the too-few precious moments we once shared together. We yearn for the past, a time when our loved ones were within reach. Without them, the world is different. The future is different. *We* are different.

We move forward slowly, tentatively, haltingly. As we begin to find our way from what once was to what now is, fresh pain blooms at unexpected moments. Without our loved ones, "someday" now means something else entirely. We mourn for what has been lost and for what might've been.

Losing Tristram was a shock. I was forty-five years old when my beloved husband died suddenly at age fifty-seven. A cancer survivor, Tris did all he could to remain healthy. He kept a strict sleep schedule. He ate mostly fruits and vegetables. On the morning of his heart attack, he'd just returned home from the gym. His internet browser revealed that he'd searched "heart attack symptoms mayo clinic." We weren't together while this was happening. I was at a coffee shop chatting with a friend who'd just told me that she was pregnant. As we sipped our lattes, Tris texted from home to let me know he'd called 911. I missed that final text, laughing and distracted by the news of my friend's impending motherhood.

Tris was dying . . . and then he was dead. We didn't get to say goodbye. He was on his own. There were the EMTs in the ambulance and the staff in the emergency room, but being with strangers isn't the same as being with the people who love you. I wasn't there to care for him, to hold his hand. I wasn't there to remind him how much we adored him. Was he afraid? Was he in pain? There's no way to know. Our time together had ended. The time we'd had wasn't nearly enough.

This incredible loss pulled me into a world full of grief and mourning, regret and confusion, disorientation and groundlessness. *The Good Widow* was borne of my attempts to make sense of what I learned in the eighteen months after my husband's unexpected death. The rawest moments of emotional complexity—which led to major shifts in my identity, roles, and relationships—are captured in this collection of personal essays.

In the first few months after Tris died, I felt numb. Denial hit hard. My initial attempts at processing this profound life change involved reading. Desperate for information, no genre was off-limits: memoir, fiction, self-help, and professional guides for clinicians like me. I became intent on understanding what had just happened. I hoped to forecast what to expect, both for me and for our family. I had no idea how to be a widow and no idea how to parent our bereaved children. When their dad died, my stepson, Jonah, was twenty-six years old and our daughter, Maddy, was fifteen.

Reading so many books, by so many different authors who'd also been impacted by grief, helped me feel less alone. And although Tris was profoundly special and unique, I soon learned that my own experience of loss wasn't particularly special or unique. In a concrete way, reading helped me focus on an obvious truth I'd initially overlooked: grief is a universal human experience that affects us all.

As the boundaries around denial began to fray, I became less numb and increasingly overwhelmed by intense, sometimes conflicting emotions. These sensations were entirely unfamiliar. Many of my behaviors were also unfamiliar. At times, I wondered about my mental health. Was I suddenly losing my mind? I barely recognized myself.

The Good Widow begins by exploring, in the Introduction, "Who am I without him?" In Parts I through III, I share personal stories of pain, of love, and of forward movement. There were times when, perhaps like you, I struggled with seemingly unbearable anguish. Perhaps also like you, I eventually found new ways to relate to those around me and to reach out to others who had experienced loss. Throughout, I forced myself to take halting steps forward, stumbling into new sources of pain and gratitude, discovering new ways to carry my past love forward, eventually developing hope for the future.

The Good Widow exists because there were times when I felt compelled to write, as if drawn by a magnetic force. Writing allowed me to release the pain and to express my inner emotional turmoil. The urge to write pulled me away from other tasks: stacks of ungraded papers, partially cooked dinners, a half-cleaned bathroom. I felt driven to find words that could make sense of the strange new world I inhabited. *What am I doing? Who am I now?* I had to find the words for what was happening in my mind, in my relationships, and in my life. Most of those words were haphazard and jumbled. Some eventually were organized into sentences which grew into paragraphs and, finally, into the essays which comprise this book.

As a new widow, I perpetually felt like a liar, a fraud, an imposter. It was as if I was only *pretending* to live a normal life. I talked with cashiers and clerks who had absolutely no idea that my heart had been shattered into bits. As I interacted with colleagues and students at the college where I teach, my despair seemed invisible. Although grief is a universal human experience, not everyone recognizes its effects. Not everyone has lost someone yet.

In the early months, when I felt isolated and invisible, reading first-person accounts of grief served as a type of compass, helping me navigate my way across a harsh new terrain. These words and sentences helped me feel less alone, less alien. When other authors described their experiences in ways that I could relate to but had not yet articulated, I felt *seen*.

Even as we travel different paths—as we move with and through the pain of loss—the outlines of our movements are familiar. There is recognition, acceptance, and more to be found in words shared among us. May the pages of this book offer you moments of clarity and connection, of healing and hope.

Jennifer Katz, PhD
Rochester, New York
February 24, 2020

Editor's Note: The essays appearing in *The Good Widow* are grouped thematically rather than chronologically. Each grouping ends with a set of related questions ("Reflecting on . . .") encouraging independent exploration.

INTRODUCTION
The Feminist Widow

My husband Tris died suddenly after we'd been married for eighteen years, two months, and two days. After the initial shock, when the world collapsed, I was flooded by disturbing thoughts. *My life is over. Who am I now?*

The identity crisis was real. I'd never before defined myself in terms of my husband or my marriage. After we wed I kept my name, my habit of self-reliance, and my love of solitude. I adored him, of course. But we had the type of marriage in which there was ample space for individual pursuits and pleasures. As academic clinical psychologists, we both had workaholic tendencies. Outside of work, Tris made daily visits to the gym and traveled all over the world. He read science magazines and collected rare coins. I did yoga and volunteered. I read almost constantly and spent time with friends. We led full individual lives, joined securely at the center—at the heart. If we were an image, we'd have been the curving, winding, figure-eight shape of infinity. We gave each other boundless love and unrestrained space for growth and movement. Many of our days were spent apart. Yet, at night, we had much to share while lying close together.

I had no idea such a marriage was possible. It was a tremendous gift.

֍

When my twin brother married his first wife, at age twenty-three, I was a harried third-year graduate student. I flew alone to Florida for the wedding where relatives oozed with disappointment. *Where's your boyfriend? Is it serious? When are you going to find a man, tie the knot?* I deflected. As the ceremony ended, my new sister-in-law threw her bouquet directly at me. I stepped back and away, the flowers landing on the floor with an awkward thud. Later, my grandmother scolded me for "ruining" this traditional ritual.

As a child, I had rejected the idea of marriage. I had witnessed two unhappy people tethered to one another by obligations and resentment. Marriage made people like my mother sacrifice their true desires and their true selves to please their partners without clear benefit. Mom was a housewife who sought fulfillment in a spotless kitchen and the perfectly folded bedsheet. The domestic sphere was a tiny place in the world where she could wield full control and competence. At the same time, marriage enabled people like my father to hunt wanton desires with careless abandon. Dad was almost never home, more apt to pursue leisure interests accompanied by young, tanned girlfriends. He rarely wore his wedding ring. The world was a huge place in which he was free to find pleasure, occasionally returning home for a hot-cooked meal and freshly laundered socks.

As a child, family and culture offered me explicit lessons in preparing for married life and its gendered expectations and obligations. I was told to avoid being "too smart" to avoid "scaring off the boys." I received specific instruction in domesticity, especially related to culinary skills: "No man will want to marry you if you don't learn to cook." I was directed to wear makeup to "look nice" for my future husband when he got home from a long day's work. Female sexual restraint was also on the menu. "Why buy the cow when you can get the milk for free?"

Yet throughout my childhood, one particular uncle persistently kissed me, open-mouthed, gagging me with his wide, slimy tongue.

When I later began refusing to kiss relatives, my parents labelled me "cold." This was the first time I grasped that my normally hyper-protective father wasn't totally invested in my safety. Once as a teen, while lathering up in the shower, I was startled to find this same uncle watching me through the bathroom window. When I complained, Dad said I was "overreacting."

Some ten years later, while walking with Dad and his own father through a parking lot, my grandfather slipped a hand down into the back pocket of my jeans. An adult in my mid-20s, I was livid. I protested loudly, as I would to anyone who behaved this way, "Get your hand off my ass!" My father reacted with alarm, but not as I expected: "Jenny! Shhh!" He was correcting me?! My anger festered into a white-hot rage.

At the time, what I thought I knew was this: *family ties are a trap.* My resolve to avoid marriage altogether crystallized.

৵৹

I met Tris about a year after the parking lot incident, a few months before finishing my graduate studies. He was interviewing me for a faculty position at the large state school where he already worked. Ultimately, I accepted the job. There were very few people in the tiny town where we then lived. There were even fewer opportunities to socialize. For these reasons, faculty members often spent time together over lunch and on the weekends. This arrangement allowed Tris and me to become friends.

Then a shift occurred.

At a faculty party held in September, he and I spent nearly the whole night talking—just the two of us. Although typically reserved, on this occasion Tris talked openly about his family and, in particular, a sister. He described concerns he had about challenges she had faced, making a connection between them and the sexism both girls and women routinely encounter. I sympathized. As we exchanged stories, I felt an unmistakable spark. He began to look at me differently. In this new gaze, I could see him taking me in, viewing me in a new light.

A mutual friend noticed this, too, and said so, "I think Tris has a crush on you." It sounded silly and I denied it, even though I knew precisely what our friend meant. I was flattered but struggled to see myself romantically involved with a man who'd been divorced, a single dad to a six-year-old child.

Tris and I began to have lunch together, just the two of us, after pretending to look for other people who might join us. With each interaction, he inspired surprising feelings in me. I was impressed with his intelligence and gentle humor. He spoke about his son, Jonah, with unrestrained affection. He observed me carefully and then used that information in thoughtful ways. Once, when I had informed him that I didn't like to waste food, he agreed, "I know." I was amazed. *How so?* When I asked, he recalled watching me attempt to peel an orange for six full minutes before giving up on the inaccessible, unripe fruit.

Like my uncle, Tris watched me. Unlike my uncle, Tris wanted to know more about me, the real me—not my exterior, my shell. He didn't demand servitude or accommodation. He seemed to delight in my voice, my laughter, my mere presence. When I was short-tempered or short-sighted, he laughed without malice. *Impatient Jenny.* When I was absent, he missed me and said so. *Fun Jenny!* He liked to bait me with incomplete song lyrics, coaxing me to sing what might be the chorus to Barry Manilow's "Copacabana." *Dancing, Singing Jenny.*

And when I complained and it mattered, Tris heard me. During my first year as a faculty member, a colleague more than thirty years my senior asked me over to his house to share a bottle of wine. A different male colleague handed me a condom in a bizarre hallway exchange. When I told Tris about these incidents, he offered to accompany me to human resources so that I could report them. I told him, "It's not worth it. It won't do any good." He gently disagreed but said it was entirely my call. I didn't report anything. But I knew that I could and that, if I did, he would be a source of validation, compassion, support, and love. *Beautiful Jenny, I love you.*

જ

Reader, I married him.

Before our marriage, I'd been content to be fully self-reliant. I lived alone, happily, in a tiny apartment with few possessions and too much yogurt in the fridge. My world was relatively small. In a fledgling career, as a new professional and assistant professor, I had no children to care for and a few hundred dollars in the bank. I also had the exterior gifts of youth: thick hair, an unlined face, speckle-free hands. Those gifts are now gone, replaced by one I hold on the interior: I know what joy true love and even marriage can bring.

I still believe marriage and family can be a trap. But Tris showed me that marriage also can be a soft place to land. Marriage can offer freedom for choices to be made and respected. Give and take can shift as we negotiate job upheavals, welcome a new baby, pursue grant deadlines, and move through periods of sickness and health. Family—if rooted in *this* type of marital bond—can be a place in which everyone is heard and valued, in which boundaries are respected, in which we give and receive help freely, in which we love without condition or limit.

Many women continue to experience marriage the way my mother did. Many women accommodate; they sacrifice time, names, careers, bodies, and desires. When a person's identity is shrouded in a marriage and that marriage then ends, through divorce or death, it makes sense for that person to experience a crisis of identity. I witnessed this with my own mother, who eventually divorced and then moved on to find mutual love.

After Tris died, I was surprised to learn that there could *still* be a crisis of identity, even when our identities were tethered yet remained separate. The person who most made my life meaningful, who helped me develop my career, who gave me children, who gently and lovingly stitched together my fragmented, mistrustful soul . . . is gone. Without him, I wonder: *Who am I now?*

Time will tell.

For now, I feel a constant, bittersweet ache. While missing my husband, I'm also grateful for how much he gave me, taught me, and opened me. I try to remain open to what might come next, open to being shaped by grief, open to renewal. I begin by expressing, through writing, my unfinished story of pain, love, and hope.

PART I
Contracting in Pain

Grief is frustrating. It leaves us with a permanently unresolved yearning, an insatiable need, an unscratchable itch. Grief is also cold. There's a chill to the lifeless body, to the loneliness of bereavement, to the icy barrenness of a new year, a new decade, without our person in the world.

Grief forced me to confront different forms of emptiness. I've faced physical emptiness: a body without a heartbeat, our half-empty bed, his unworn slacks. I've faced emotional emptiness. Without my husband, my children and I crave the love and support he once provided. And I've faced spiritual emptiness, too, wondering who I am and who I'm to become. *What's the point, really, of anything?*

The following essays describe the pain of grief. That pain manifested in a literal aching of the heart and a chronic tensing of muscles. I was forced to adapt and change, learning to bear the unbearable and to stop resisting the new reality of a life I didn't choose—and definitely didn't want.

The End

My husband, Tris, died on a Monday morning.
We hadn't actually spoken that day. His alarm went off at the usual time: 6:30 a.m. I vaguely remember reaching out to him and stroking his lower back and hip. The light was dim. I closed my eyes and fell back asleep.

We'd had a lovely final weekend together. He had been away on a work trip to California and took a red eye flight home Friday night. I stayed up much too late on Friday so that I, too, would be overtired. It worked. We napped together for almost four hours. We then drove over to the gym, where I biked while he lifted weights and used the elliptical machine. Sweaty, we sat in the home office for our weekly Skype meeting with our oldest child, Jonah, now living in New York City. Tris was interested in Jonah's updates but was undeniably sleepy, eyelids fluttering. *My poor man.* I suggested that I take him and our youngest child, Maddy, out to dinner to celebrate his homecoming. Eyes widening with mild surprise and appreciation, Tris responded with a shy, sweet smile: "That would be so nice."

I drove. We dined on Asian fusion but, before we were even close to done, Maddy begged for frozen custard dessert. We agreed—on the condition that immediately afterward she'd join us to watch a movie, *A Few Good Men.* On a recent vacation, our family had toured and spent the night at a military academy, inspiring us to share this classic film with her. She agreed but grew bored as soon as the custard was gone, so we told her to run along and that we'd call her back for the major, climactic scene. Tris and I were *not* bored. We sat closely together on our yellow couch, hands intertwined, enthralled with the quick pacing and speedy dialogue. The scenes packed a powerful punch. We paused the film long enough to fetch Maddy before Jack Nicholson growled, "You can't handle the truth!" It was thrilling. It was also funny. Tris loved to use that same phrase, in a joking way, in everyday conversations. This was our own inside joke.

The next morning, Tris had a busy day. He went to the grocery store and the farmer's market, as he always did. He brought home flowers for me, as he always did. But he also went to the lab for a blood test and took Maddy to a local arts festival and to the Verizon store where he purchased a new iPhone and iPad. "Hello, Siri. Hello," Tris greeted his new devices, introducing them to the sound of his voice. He also managed phone calls and emails. From my lazy perch on the red couch, devouring a wonderful new novel, I'd periodically see and hear Tris and Maddy between errands—entering and leaving, chatting and laughing.

My library book was a great distraction from the upcoming week. Tris had a major medical procedure scheduled for Tuesday morning. I was nervous, jumpy, and tense. His medical history included a bone marrow transplant. This was after chemotherapy and radiation were used to treat a cancerous, football-sized tumor in his chest. These interventions had destroyed much of his lung and heart tissue. About three years before our last weekend together, he had suffered a heart attack and had been diagnosed with heart failure.

Ever responsible and capable, Tris had rallied by being scrupulous about diet and exercise. Despite his efforts, he had suffered from various ailments. Most recently, his lung had collapsed. An initial scan showed no lung tumors, which was a huge relief, but on Tuesday he was scheduled to have the fluid drained and the lung biopsied. The oncologist wanted it done sooner rather than later. Her urgency concerned me. The procedure wasn't complex, nor was it particularly dangerous. But there was risk because Tris's blood didn't always clot. In fact, we now had a regular routine for spending the night in the ER with his bloody nose. I had catastrophic thoughts about Tuesday and purposefully scheduled work-related meetings on Monday to free up time later in the week. *Just in case*, I thought.

When I expressed my worries, Tris gently teased me. It was fortunate for our relationship that he'd always found my catastrophic thinking to be more amusing than irritating. He told me the procedure would go well. He told me that he went for Sunday's blood test to ensure it would be safe to drain the lung. He told me that he was confident the biopsy results would show that there was no reason to worry. Yet my anxiety persisted; I couldn't be calmed by his even, reassuring tone. This was our general pattern in dealing with his health problems. He was tranquil, and I was terrified. Rinse, repeat.

Tris made us a delicious final dinner. He roasted corn on the cob from the farmer's market and assembled a salad of lettuce, shaved almonds, blue cheese, and his famous oil and vinegar dressing. He was a creative cook, always offering us wonderful seasonal foods. After dinner, we all watched a movie, *Meet the Parents*. Tris and I had seen this comedy many years ago, back when we'd been dating. Recently, Maddy had begun her first romantic relationship. Our confident, steady girl had been so uncharacteristically nervous about making a good impression on her new boyfriend's parents that we'd been inspired to share this film with her. The three of us laughed at the antics, especially at the cat who'd been clicker trained to use the toilet instead of a litter box. This was familiar. Tris and Maddy had attempted to clicker train our cat, Pumpkin, a few years back.

Maddy enjoyed the film and concluded that meeting her boyfriend's parents wasn't nearly as bad as it could've been. We laughed at this. We took a break for frozen yogurt and fresh berries. As he routinely did, Tris impishly referred to the berries with silly names.

Strawberries were *strawbs and* blueberries were *bluebs.* Bellies full, we returned to the yellow couch to finish laughing together in front of our TV. Then Maddy said goodnight and went to bed.

Tris and I both checked our email and the news, still sitting on the yellow coach. That was our typical routine. Ever since the 2016 presidential election, at least one of us checked the news before bed to learn what new outrageous event had taken place. I told Tris that I had read that President Trump was going to appoint Steven Segal to be the new Russian ambassador. Tris burst out laughing, saying something like, "Well, that'll certainly solve all of our problems with Russia."

We ambled upstairs to get ready for bed. By the time I exited the bathroom, he was already under the covers, facing the windows. He must've still been tired from his trip. In our regular sleep position, he was the little spoon, and I was the big spoon pressed against his back. That final night, we slept as we always did: big spoon over little, my left arm around his waist, clutching his left thumb. Until 6:30 a.m.

When I fully woke up the next morning, after Tris had already left, it was about 7:00 a.m. I checked on Maddy. We had plans to go out to an early breakfast. At the restaurant, we ordered crepes and talked about her friend group. One of the trio was feeling left out. I listened and offered advice after she showed me text messages on her phone. She was hoping to hear back from a friend who hadn't yet responded to her last text, hopeful that all would be resolved. We left breakfast and headed to a coffee shop where I had a meeting set up at 10:00 a.m. We were a few minutes early, so I took Maddy to get a haircut. I waited in the salon, playing a game on my phone. At some point, I told Maddy to come meet me a few doors down at the coffee shop. I didn't want to be late. Then I put my phone on silent.

In the coffee shop, I sat with a former student, by now a friend and colleague, who had recently graduated with her doctorate. It was wonderful to catch up. I was thrilled to hear that she was pregnant and due in December. We turned to work. During the fall, she would be teaching a class I had once taught her many years ago. I happily offered her books, materials, and inside knowledge about the workings of our department. Maddy joined us, hair freshly trimmed. We all sipped drinks and chatted. As our conversation drew to an end, we decided to set up a regular weekly meeting, and I pulled out my phone to check my schedule.

My focus immediately shifted. There were multiple missed calls and a voicemail. There were also several unread texts. The most recent one, from Tris, was visible: "May be having heart attack. Called 911. Ambulance on the way." I jumped out of my chair, knocking items over. "We have to go," I told Maddy loudly, urgently. People stared. I didn't care. My friend looked alarmed, "Is everything okay?" "Yes. No. I don't know. I'm sorry. We have to go. My husband is in the hospital." She said, "Go, I'll clean up." I rushed out to the car with Maddy and started driving to the emergency room. We listened to a voicemail from our housekeeper who said Tris had been taken to the hospital. I barked orders: "Text Daddy—tell him we're on our way to him. Call home and ask if we're going to the right place." Our housekeeper confirmed the hospital's location, adding: "Drive slow. Be safe."

As we drove toward the hospital, I was already planning our arrival. I told Maddy that I'd drop her at the entrance. She was to go inside and find her dad right away. Then I'd park the car and join her as soon as I could. She agreed. Neither of us wanted him to be alone. I turned into the now-familiar hospital driveway and ushered her out of the car: "Go in that door," I pointed, "and I'll meet you two ASAP." She nodded and got out. I turned into the parking garage and paused to grab a ticket. The garage was crowded. I couldn't find a space. Waves of frustration and dread washed over me. Why weren't there any spaces?! I climbed up, up, the circular structure, looking for a place to leave my car. My heart pounded; my breath caught.

I saw a space . . . and drove past it.

Immediately, I shook myself. What had I just done? Was I avoiding a potential horrible new reality? I realized, with horror, that this might be the last peaceful moment of my life. Just as suddenly, I realized I had just sent our fifteen-year-old daughter, *alone*, to be with her father—her father, who might be dying, might have died, might be dead. I became frantic. I swerved into the very next available space and jogged out of the parking structure. Outside, the bright morning sun was blinding.

Maddy was waiting in the back of the ER, standing near a podium where people go to check on ER patients. While a woman argued with the staff member at the podium, I asked Maddy what had happened. "They wouldn't tell me anything until you got here," she reported. Along with my fears and my worries about Tris, still alone, I was flooded with gratitude that there were rules and procedures in place to protect children from their thoughtless parents.

As soon as the staff member was free, I asked about Tris. She brought us to a tiny room packed with too many chairs. Kindly, she told us the doctor would be in to talk to us shortly. Immediately after sitting, I felt my bladder strain. I needed to pee, badly. *The coffee*, I thought stupidly. "I drank too much coffee," I told Maddy, who also needed a restroom. But we didn't move. We sat side by side, clutching hands. I told her that this might be very bad. And that, no matter what, it would be okay, and we would be together. She told me that she knew. We waited. I felt the pressure in my bladder as keenly as I felt the pressure rising in my chest. *This is absolutely unbearable*, I thought. *Can I bear this?*

A woman entered the room with a clipboard and a checklist, "I just have a few questions for you." She asked me to verify Tris's address and cell phone number. She had all of these answers on a printout, checking them off as I mechanically recited the same information listed on the clipboard. She asked me about his other emergency contact, Tris's sister. *Yes, yes.* She asked if there were any other emergency contacts to add. I hesitated, about to mention Jonah's name, before saying, "No." She checked on our insurance and other final details, thanked me, and said the doctor would be in soon.

This seemed like an excellent sign. *Tris must be in the ICU,* I thought. Why else would they need his cell phone number? Why else would they need updated emergency contact information? I told Maddy that I thought this was a promising development. She agreed and asked if I had been about to tell them to add Jonah as another emergency contact. I was impressed. She read me so well! The intense pressure in my chest lessened. I seriously considered finding a restroom before they took us to the ICU to see Tris. Instead, frozen in my seat, I didn't move.

Eventually, a man and a woman entered the room. The man was a medical resident. The woman was a social worker. The resident asked who we were in relation to Tris. I told him, and he nodded.

Then he said he was sorry but Tris had died. He seemed to have had a heart attack. They were unable to revive him although they had tried everything they could. I could hear the resident clearly—but his words sounded like they were coming from inside a tunnel, far away. What about the ICU? My brain struggled to process this information as my heart shattered into a million sharp fragments.

Outwardly, I was calm. Inside, I felt chaos. My first question was: "Can we see him?" The resident said yes, though it might be a few minutes and it might be unpleasant. That they would have to "clean him up." *Yes, yes, fine.* I was both thankful and desperate to see him. It was confusing to feel relieved to have the opportunity to see my dead husband's body. Truly, the world had turned upside down.

I asked if Tris might be a candidate for organ donation. I said that the donation people might not want his organs because they seemed to be in bad shape, but that I knew he'd want to offer. The social worker thanked me (us?) and said that the organ donation office would be in touch. At some point, the resident left the room. I told the social worker that Jonah was in New York City. He might want to see his dad, but I didn't know for sure. If he did, would that be possible? The social worker was reassuring, saying that this wouldn't be a problem if Jonah could come soon.

The social worker turned to leave. Maddy and I followed her out, finding a restroom. Everything seemed surreal. My mind was racing with thoughts about Jonah. *I have to call Jonah. He needs to come home.* With shaking hands, I dialed his number. He answered with a question in his voice, confused that I would call mid-morning on a Monday, violating our normal Saturday routine. Calmly, I told him to please sit down. Then I thought, *Oh, no, he knows. So I need to tell him.* Before he could actually sit, I told him that his father had a heart attack and had died. I was so sorry. He cried out and then he was sobbing. It was excruciating. I told him to just come, come as soon as he could. Bring his girlfriend, if he could. Just get on the next plane and come home. "Wait—what happened again, exactly?" Jonah asked. It was a heart attack, and they did everything they could to save him. It wasn't enough. Come. Just come.

Maddy and I sat together. I felt incredibly overwhelmed by having inflicted this pain on Jonah. How truly terrible to deliver that kind of devastating news. And I didn't do it well. He was in so much pain. I reeled. Maddy nudged me: "You need to call Aunt Lisa. She's his sister. She deserves to know."

"I know," I told her. "I just don't want to." We paused.

"Mom, you have to," Maddy insisted. "It's the right thing to do."

"I know," I repeated, sitting motionless. "I will. I just need a minute." There was another pause. Maddy looked at me impatiently. "Okay," I said, still not moving. Finally, I called. It was just like the call to Jonah. I told her. She cried out. She sobbed. She asked questions, confused. *How? What? When? Wait—what?!* I tried to explain. It was horrific. I can't actually remember the rest.

Here, everything is jumbled. We kept waiting in the tiny room. Jonah called back to ask if he would be able to see his dad's body. I reassured him that was the plan. I was determined to see Tris as soon as possible. We waited and waited. I needed the restroom again. Finally, the social worker came to get us. I stood immediately but Maddy balked. I said that I'd go first and make sure it was okay. I didn't want Maddy to be traumatized if her dad's body was wrecked. But I knew Maddy wasn't squeamish about bodies. My ninety-two-year-old grandmother had died the summer before. Unlike many others at the funeral, Maddy was unfazed by the viewing, by seeing her body laid out in the coffin. Now, though, Maddy looked very unsure. I told her I'd return to tell her how he looked, to let her know if it would be okay.

The social worker led me into a room. Tris lay on his back on a bed, covered by a sheet. A small trickle of blood had dried on his lower lip. He was still and lifeless, yet his hands were still warm and his hair was still soft. I held one of his hands and stroked his silky forehead hair. I didn't cry. I wanted to really be present during what might be our last few moments together. "I'm so sorry," I told him. "I wasn't here. Were you scared? I should've been with you. I'm so sorry. I love you. You are the love of my life. I love you forever. I'm so sorry."

Looking down at his hand, I noticed puncture marks from an IV. There were also puncture marks on the side of his neck. *His poor body.* The violence of resuscitation lingered. He had been through so much. I was torn, not wanting to leave him but also not wanting to leave Maddy in the waiting room, alone, thinking about how her father had just died. I whispered one last, "I love you," and returned to our daughter, clutching the plastic bag which held his wedding ring and cell phone.

Maddy looked uncertain when I told her that her Daddy looked okay, not great, and that it might be helpful to say goodbye. She remained unsure. I suggested she try seeing him. Maddy followed me back to the room. I was confused, disoriented, unsure which door to open. After we found the correct room, Maddy peered inside from the doorway and immediately fled. I ran after her. There would be no more time with Tris.

Back again in the tiny waiting room, the social worker asked me if I'd be able to drive home. I heard myself say, "Yes," while wondering if this was true. Instead, I asked her who to call when Jonah arrived so that he could see his dad. She wrote down the number on a piece of pink notebook paper. Then she handed me a ticket for free parking. Thoughts of Monopoly flashed through my brain. Then Maddy and I left the hospital, with me pushing the up button on the elevator when where we really needed was to go down.

We climbed into the car and slowly drove down in circles toward the exit. The man at the payment booth smiled widely at us. "How's your day?" he asked cheerfully. I grasped that the world had ended but no one knew. It was only our world. Everyone else was still living their lives, moving through their days. "We're doing okay," I managed, while handing him our ticket. We drove home, slowly, never veering from the right-hand lane. It felt like being under water, in a fog, or in one of those nightmares where your body feels stiff and frozen. Every motion took so much effort.

We got home and entered the house. Tris's new cell phone had been ringing. A close work colleague had been calling. Tris hadn't showed up to a meeting, which was totally unlike him, so she was concerned. I called her back, by now knowing what to expect from this third phone call. I broke the news. She cried out. She sounded confused and disoriented. *What? How? When? Wait—what?!*

I tried to explain and said I was sorry. I asked her to tell others at work. I didn't want to call anyone else. I just wanted to be with Maddy and in our house, the place where we had built a life, a family, a home.

A random thought struck me. We needed sealable plastic bags

to store his clothing, his smell. I looked. There weren't any bags in the drawer. "What should we do?" I asked, suddenly devious. "What about the house where you're pet sitting? Don't they have any bags? We could break into their house and steal their bags."

It was a plan. We walked down the street to our neighbor's house. It felt strangely hot and sunny. *Maybe I should wear a hat,* I thought dumbly. *Or sunglasses. This glare is unbelievable. I can't believe how bright and hot the world is.*

We entered our neighbor's kitchen and found one bag. We took it and the box it came in. I promised we'd replace it later. We went home and I bagged a T-shirt. But there were more. We needed *more* bags.

I knew that when I picked up the phone to call someone it would change everything. Maddy would withdraw. And Tris would really be dead. I wanted to put it off. But at some point, I couldn't any longer. We urgently needed plastic bags. Also, we needed to do other things, important things, although I didn't know how to figure out what those things might be.

I consulted a book on my shelf, *Checklists for Life*. I looked up the section on what to do when someone dies. "Call a supportive friend," the book advised. It's first on the list. So I did.

The Saddest Thing

A few months after Tris died, our daughter Maddy asked, "What makes you the most sad about Daddy's death?"

I don't know exactly how we got to the place where she asked me this question. We had just finished dinner. Maddy had commented on my poor appetite, which had been suppressed by a constant sense of frustration and dread. The anxiety that began on the frantic drive to the hospital—the tension that escalated in the little room where we waited to hear about Tris's death—never left. Rather, tentacles of pain traveled down to my inner core and rooted. From these roots, like a set of fiery blood-red buds, anguish bloomed and multiplied. Grief literally felt like heartbreak.

On the day Tris died, three months and three days before this conversation, his death had seemed like the worst possible thing, the saddest thing. But by the time Maddy posed her question, I had grown to understand that what happened on that day was just the start of the worst possible thing: Tris's non-existence. Stupidly, I had misunderstood and underestimated grief. There was an event. My beloved died. Later, it became clearer that the event merely signaled a new life ahead, a new way of living. I felt violently torn and divided, pulled back into the past while also unwillingly wrenched forward into a bleak and barren future.

Back to the question. I told Maddy that, for me, the saddest part of grief was the perpetual sense of loss. All of the realizations about what Tris and I would never share again. Our favorite restaurant. Our guilty pleasure TV shows. Her orchestra concerts. Voting night. Wine tasting. Unexpected good news. Also, happy times from the past now were recast with the bittersweet tang of finality. The last photo I had taken of his happy, smiling face. The last time we celebrated Father's Day. The last gift he had given to me. Each new realization demanded acknowledgement. Each demanded space and energy for mourning. Some were absolutely overwhelming.

Maddy nodded, face flushed. Although she was normally so sturdy, so stoic, unshed tears shone in her eyes. It took her some effort to say what her saddest thing was. She began with reassurance, by saying that she didn't blame me, that it wasn't my fault. She wasn't mad. Still, the thing that made her "the most sad" was this: I hadn't answered the phone when Daddy called to say goodbye.

I was stunned. Unspoken words flashed through my brain: *Wait— what? Had he called to say goodbye?*

I snapped to attention. My verbal response was immediate. I told Maddy that I didn't think he had called to say goodbye. He had texted. He didn't call. Also, I told her this: If Daddy thought it was the end, then, yes, he would've called Jonah and also her. He'd have left a voicemail saying, "I love you." But that's not what he did. That's not what he said. The final text message he sent wasn't a goodbye: "May be having heart attack. Called 911. Ambulance on the way."

I repeated this essential point. His final text message communicated no certainty about the end. Even more importantly, I told her, it's not clear whether it would've been better for Daddy to have us there or not. If we were there, he'd have worried about us. I asked if it would've been better to be there in the ambulance or at the hospital, watching him in his final moments. I pointed out that this could be scary for him and also for us. He had died suddenly, unpredictably. There would be no way for us to be prepared and calm enough to sadly hold his hand and tell him to let go when he's ready. That's what a dying person would need. But given the suddenness of the end, without any type of warning, there was no way that we could be ready to do that.

Still, it was clear Maddy had regret. This was understandable, even if she misremembered or misunderstood actual events. She had regret for what had *not* happened.

I asked, "Was the saddest thing not being able to say goodbye?" She said it was.

I reassured my now sobbing girl that our family's love was deep and unshakeable, unaffected by bad moods or bad days. Her daddy was steady, secure, unflagging. So were we. Her daddy didn't need to say goodbye to know how much we loved him. We knew. He knew. She nodded.

I reminded her of our last day together. The two of them went to an art festival and the three of us had dinner, then frozen yogurt with berries for dessert. We watched a comedy and we laughed—fully content, fully sharing joy and love. Maddy sobbed, tears dripping down her cheeks and chin. Her nose ran. My heart broke.

I asked our daughter, "If we could go back and control what happened that day, even if Daddy still had to die that morning, what would we want to have happen?"

We decided that he would've gone out to breakfast with the two of us. We decided that he'd still have had the chest pains which got him to call 911. But instead of calling an ambulance himself, I would've driven him to the hospital. We decided that he would have been with us for most of the morning. We would've had time to express love and appreciation, the final expressions we weren't able to offer on the actual, real day.

Then I suggested that Daddy wouldn't have wanted us to be in the room with him when his heart suddenly gave out. He wouldn't have wanted us to see that. It could be a terrible final last moment together, a shocking and horrific last memory seared into our brains.

So instead, in this fantasy death, we would've left the room to buy him a snack. We would've gone to a vending machine to get a Snickers candy bar, or maybe potato chips. He had loved chocolate and salty treats but wasn't allowed to have them anymore. When we left, he would slip away happy with anticipation—secure in being loved and cared for by his girls.

In reality, on the day of his death, my own memory of our last moment together is hazy. Tris's alarm went off at 6:30 a.m., as it did every morning. He paused, seated on the edge of our bed, feet on the floor. I stirred and reached out to caress his lower back, giving him a gentle stroke, a soft pat-pat. Then I turned over and fell back asleep.

That was the end. This was my last memory of him being alive. There were no words, just a hazy moment, half-awake. Our last touch. It isn't enough.

But Maddy didn't have even that.

Dreams and Destruction

I found myself walking through life in a dreamlike state. The chronic, relentless fatigue was oddly familiar, not unlike my experience of mothering an infant who had stubbornly refused to sleep. Almost six months after Tris's passing, I felt like I somehow *was* that infant. Rather than simply a state of being, exhaustion had become a part of my personhood, my essence. Exhaustion was shaping me, fundamental to my new self.

Dreams felt dangerous. Once I dreamed of Tris. The funeral had all been a mistake. He'd been away, but now he'd returned. I was thrilled to see him! After we hugged and kissed, the two of us settled together on the yellow couch, our hands linked, content to be together.

When I woke, I sobbed.

Once I dreamed of a woman who told me she'd help me cope with grief. She stood above me, speaking, as I passively reclined on a chair like one used by the dentist. With circular motions, she spread viscous white lotion on my cheeks. As I wondered why this was happening, she suddenly pulled up the sides of a shiny silver plastic container all around my body. Zipping me inside, she told me it would help. *It was for the best.*

I jolted awake, heart pounding.

The waking hours weren't much better. There seemed to be no actual waking from this nightmare. Still, at night—like an infant—I resisted sleep. I resisted dreams. Friends suggested exercise and essential oils, melatonin and meditation. None were safe. None would make the bed less empty. None would keep the dreams away.

Sometimes actual life felt surreal, like a living nightmare. There was no escape.

҉

One afternoon I decided to order a T-shirt quilt. I wanted Tris's shirts, sewn together, to wrap around me. I placed my order on the website and then received detailed instructions, which included this: *Cut the shirts at the seams before you send them to us. Do not send whole shirts. Sides only.*

I stared dumbly. *Really? But how?!* Cutting seemed violent, obscene. I felt protective. After all, these same shirts once lay on his skin, near his heart.

I didn't want to cut the shirts. But I didn't know what else to do. Torn, I asked our daughter for permission. She was matter-of-fact. She was sturdy. She was herself: "Well, if they want you to cut them, you should do it. It's fine, Mom."

I nodded, trying to allow her words to sink in. *It's fine, it's fine, it's fine.*

Nothing was fine, clearly, but somehow this must be. Resigned, I sat on top of our bed with the shirts stacked, scissors in hand. I began to cut. I tugged and tore away at the first shirt, separating the shoulder seam from the collar and down the side. Then I started at the bottom side and cut my way up to the sleeve. The fabric separated more easily than I had expected. It was curiously easy.

Simple and total destruction can occur in only a moment, despite a permanent effect.

I cried. Then I destroyed three shirts after stroking their softness, murmuring apologies, leaking tears.

The fourth shirt stopped me in my tracks. This was the shirt I had bought him on our honeymoon. This particular shirt felt so soft. After eighteen years, its tan color had faded. There was a small hole in the shoulder. The word *Venezia* appeared over the breastbone in brown script. It was worn, well-used, well-loved.

Sometimes life is surreal, like a dream or fantasy so sad or so sweet that it can't be believed.

Our honeymoon was another time when living had a dreamlike quality. I kept pinching myself. *I'm married. I'm in Venice. I'm in Florence. I'm so happy. How can this be possible? This can't be real.* I bought the shirt for my new husband after a benign misunderstanding. He had bought me a gift and hung it by its bag on the hanger of my dress. Hurriedly dressing for dinner, I didn't notice the bag. His plan wasn't working. My new husband pointed at the bag, "What is that?" I dismissed him, "I don't know, but it isn't mine."

His face fell. He looked so dejected, so crushed, that I finally caught on. Belatedly, I realized my new husband had generously tried to surprise me with a random gift. Because I had failed to grasp this, I came dangerously close to abandoning a white gold necklace in a hotel closet. Chastened, I donned the necklace and vowed to buy him a memento, as well, so we could always remember this magical time.

Sitting on our bed, now alone, I sobbed. Then I wiped away the tears. I sat up straight, composing myself. And then I destroyed the tan Venetian T-shirt. My beloved no longer needed a memento of our magical honeymoon.

There were eight more shirts to go. And there were no more tears left.

Bone Cold

A storm descended. The sky was dark. Our home was buried and isolated, glimmering dangerously with sharp ice. The cold was unbearable. Numb and rigid in the freezing temperature, my shaking body felt tense and empty. My hollow heart was frozen. I couldn't absorb heat or light.

Tris died in August, six months earlier. Despite the warmth of the late summer sun, his fingertips were blue-gray from poor circulation. His hands and feet were always cold. During the three years before his death, Tris was on a severely restricted diet. He refused salt, fat, and sugary desserts. He exercised daily, pushing himself relentlessly. He shrunk, his shoulders and belly receding. Newly bony and concave, Tris bought new, smaller clothes without clearing out the old ones. When he died, more than seventy shirts of varying sizes hung in the closet.

After Tris died, I became cold in every sense of the word. Icy hardness spread across my body, inside my mind. I hated my new life. I hated living without him. I even hated myself.

I shivered but did not cover up. Physical pain must be tolerated. Emotional pain must be tolerated. This new life must be endured. Rigidly, I refused potential escapes: anti-anxiety pills, alcohol, melatonin. The heated blanket remained at room temperature. I avoided my empty bed until I literally fell into it, no longer able to stand.

Tris could no longer soften, relax, unfold into a warm sleep. So why should I?

The coldness permeated my gaze. I stared at myself in the mirror, comparing my old widow self to memories of my young unmarried self, almost two decades younger. With a strange mix of anger and detachment, I observed my hollow eyes and wrinkled skin. My hair was falling out. I observed my gray pallor and fleshy rolls of fat. I was repulsed. Hardened, I craved bone. I wanted to calcify. My fingers prodded my hip bones, my ribs.

My inner masochist unfurled. I began to refuse to eat, to refuse to nourish my traitorous body with food. Tris didn't eat much and couldn't eat as a dead person. So why should I? Weak and disoriented, I savored the hollow feeling of hunger. It was a perverse victory. There was no way to feed or fill the emptiness inside me. I surrendered to deprivation, prideful and dizzy. I fastened tight, itchy, black chokers around my neck. I forced my wedding ring down a different, thicker finger. I tucked my breasts into overly tight bras and cinched my waist into overly tight pants. Angry red marks flared around my flesh. I kept myself painfully contained, intact. At times, it was hard to breathe. This felt correct.

Over time, my body contracted. As I got smaller, the elastic also gave way. There was slightly more room.

Tris would not approve but I didn't care. He wasn't here anymore. He was gone forever: cremated, destroyed by angry red flames, leaving only dust and bits of bone. There's almost nothing left.

Attempting to leave our house, I tried to shovel a path out. I slipped and fell hard on the ice. I rose, then brushed myself off and tried to take the next step.

Love Letter Number One

Dearest Tris,

Beloved, I'm in a new grief group. The first homework assignment is to write you a letter. Part of me feels like you already know everything that's gone on since you passed away. I can feel you with me. At the old grief group, I could feel your eyebrows raise in response to outrageousness. When I interact with someone who is unkind, I can feel you shaking your head.

You're here, inside my heart. Each day, every day, I carry your love and your light, your smile and your generosity. And I try to share these gifts, these gifts you gave me. I listen more attentively and with greater care. Sometimes I bask in the warmth reflected back when I hug people tighter.

There is only love. Why did I ever think that anything else mattered?

I'm a mess of contradictions: fragile yet invulnerable, myopic yet clear-eyed, exhausted yet driven. I'm raw, wounded—yet stronger than I ever knew I could be. I'm bearing the unbearable, savoring the sweetness of memories despite the acrid metallic tang of loss. I'm missing your voice, your smile, your lips.

It's been just over six months. I'm doing so much worse. The shock and disbelief have mostly faded. Reality has sunk into my bones, having pierced my flesh, my heart, my most tender self. I'm an emotional amputee. You're now a phantom limb.

You're gone and yet you're still here, with me, forever. It's not enough. But somehow it has to be.

Your Jenny

Shell

On two occasions, I spent time with my husband's lifeless body. But what remained wasn't really him. He was gone. And I, like him, became a shell of my former self.

Earlier on the first day, I was with our fifteen-year-old daughter, Maddy. We were in a coffee shop talking with a friend from my work. As I reached for my phone, text messages flashed across the screen. My husband had been taken by ambulance to the hospital. Startled, hearts racing, Maddy and I immediately left for the ER. Driving, I squinted at the hot bright sun. Electric panic sparked deep in my gut.

Maddy and I waited together in the terrible little room off the side of the emergency department—a tiny, austere room with bare walls and too many chairs. This was a room in plain sight that I'd never before noticed. In the room with too many chairs, we waited. My left hand clutched the smaller right hand of our daughter. The waiting was unbearable. A cold, intense, gnawing sensation roiled my gut. The tension was building and rising. I wondered, vaguely, *Am I about to have a panic attack?* I told Maddy that everything would be okay— no matter what. No matter what, we were together. She nodded. It was true. But it was also a tremendous lie.

Medical chart note: The 57 year old came to the ER with chest pain, altered mental status. Upon initial evaluation the patient was ashen and gray. Almost immediately the patient lost pulses and CPR was started immediately. IV access was obtained through a peripheral IV in his hand as well as a shoulder IO. Patient was intubated for airway protection successfully without complications.

Patient underwent 17 rounds of CPR, 7 doses of 1 mg IV epinephrine and 3 boluses of bicarbonate. Patient's rhythm was PEA throughout the entire resuscitation and lost pulses every time CPR was stopped.

Patient never regained any mental status.

Patient's time of death was 11:19 a.m.

In this room, we learned that Tris had died. We didn't get to say goodbye. We didn't get to say how much we loved each other. But he knew. We knew.

Medical chart note: The family was updated in a quiet room with me and alongside social worker who helped answer all questions that the family may have had. The patient was brought over so that the family could see him privately.

The ER physician was both apologetic and matter-of-fact. He was trying to be kind. Even in that moment, while I was processing information as if in a faraway echoing tunnel, I could see how awkward and awful this part of his job must be. He told us that the medical team had tried to revive my husband for more than forty minutes. They did everything that they could. Tris was altered but awake in the ambulance. The medical team was ready for him, prepared with a special unit for these types of cardiac cases. But as soon as Tris entered the ER unit, he collapsed.

When I heard this, it struck me as oddly appropriate, in keeping with Tris's character. No one was more conscientious and considerate. Tris fought for as long as he could to live. It seemed he also found a way to fight to hang on until arriving at the hospital. He would've waited for us if he could. Or maybe not. Maybe he wouldn't want this to be our last memory of him.

The physician had a few questions. One was, "Do you want an autopsy?" *No.* What would be the point of that? Hadn't he been through enough? Would it bring him back? The physician also asked, "Do you have any questions?" *YES. WHEN CAN I SEE HIM???*

The need was intensely physical. There's no way that I could've predicted how strong this need would be. I thought briefly of people whose loved ones went missing. How could they bear it? I could not bear even this. Although they promised I could see him, they said it would take a while. The staff would need to "clean him up." *Fine.* I could wait. As it turned out, apparently, I could endure anything.

When the social worker led me to the room—to be alone with him—I walked with purpose, without hesitation. It was surreal. This was, literally, a living nightmare. The words from the physician settled deeper into my brain, wedging under my flesh. This wasn't a mistake, a mix-up, or a misunderstanding. This body, this shell, was proof.

My husband's face was immobile, his expression opaque. He didn't look peaceful, exactly, although he was no longer in pain. I worried about how scared he might've been. But he didn't look scared. He looked *blank.* He was absent, gone. His hair was still soft, and his hands were still warm. I stroked his hair and kissed one of his hands, trying to soften the impact of compressions and chemicals that had failed to save him.

That night, alone in bed, I felt haunted by images of Tris's blank, lifeless face. These images felt seared into my brain, accompanied by a phrase that repeated on an endless loop: *he's not here, not here, not here, not here, not here, not here, not here . . .*

The next morning, we followed the social worker's instructions and set up a time to bring Jonah, my stepson, to the hospital to see his dad. Jonah had taken the first available flight into town. A dear family friend drove us to the hospital. We sat, tensely, waiting.

Finally, the social worker appeared, apologetic. There'd been a mix-up. Momentarily, I panicked. Would Jonah *not* be able to see his dad? The social worker clarified that the body had already been taken to the funeral home. Our family friend was angry, but I was flooded with relief. *Where* the viewing happened didn't matter; *whether* this viewing happened was what mattered. The body was all there was left.

At the funeral home, the director apologized. She suggested we meet about the arrangements before viewing the body. But I resisted. She was probably right; it made sense to have the funeral details carefully selected and planned, numbers estimated, rituals identified. Hers was a rational plan. We should be clear-eyed. But I was rigid, in every way. First, we needed to see the body, even though it was now just a shell. That's what we were supposed to do now, I sensed, before anything else.

My stepson went first. Alone, he entered the quiet parlor with navy carpet and dim lighting. Hovering outside the door, I listened to Jonah visit his dad's body. He keened. My broken heart fragmented once again.

After Jonah emerged, I took my turn. My husband lay in a coffin, no longer in a hospital bed. And he was different. His hair no longer felt soft. His skin felt icy. There was something peach colored on his face. *Is that makeup?* I was horrified to realize that, since yesterday, he had been stored in a freezer and then made "presentable."

This time, I didn't like brushing my fingers through his hair. This time, I didn't like holding his hand. I didn't kiss him again. I began to grasp that this was the first step in the new distance between us. Time would carry me forward—farther and farther away from his physical body, his existence. It was already doing so.

Maddy didn't want to see her dad's shell. I respected that but I also worried: would she later feel regret? This was a now or never moment in her young life. After some hesitation, I took two photos of my dead husband's cold, slightly made-up face. It felt very wrong. Also, it seemed like the right thing to do.

෨෨

As I wrote these words, tears fell and my chest tightened. I realized that I, too, had become a shell. The cliché is that time heals all wounds, and experts advise that the first three months after a death are often the worst time. But that wasn't my experience. About six months after Tris's death, I found myself getting worse—much, much worse—not better.

I read books about grieving and how to grieve. I attended a grief group that began just a few weeks after Tris's death. There are two main tasks of grief work, I learned, and they feel somewhat contradictory. One task is to process the feelings and make meaning from the loss. The other task is to learn to live a new life in which your loved one is physically absent. Experts advise spending some time on both tasks on most days. Being prone to denial, rather than processing feelings, my preferred grief task was learning to live a new life. In the immediate aftermath, I managed by putting one foot in front of the other. Pay the tax bill. Take out the garbage. Floss. I took tiny faltering steps, trying not to look up or too far ahead, keeping focus on one chore and one day at a time. Declutter the linen closet, the stack of Tupperware, the collection of winter boots. Shop, cook, feed the family. Tris had been the one to shop, to prepare meals and nourish us. But this was now my new responsibility.

At first, I cried periodically but quietly—almost never when I was alone. The grief was too deep for tears and too profound to actually touch. Occasionally, though, random events set it off, including my own internal ideas or perceptions. When I read an article he'd find interesting or received good news, I'd be silently ambushed with the inability to share with him.

The new semester had begun two weeks after Tris died. So I went to work. Working was helpful. I was distracted, less focused on my loss and worry for my children. Gamely, I attended to tasks that could be completed, marked with a check, or crossed off a list. None of this seemed to really matter, of course, but it was something to do, a way forward. The distracted mind can fool everyone, even me. *Nothing to see here, folks. I'm fine, really—mostly, probably. I'm just . . . slightly foggy.*

Initially, there was a clear boundary. I was sad at home and fine at work. Going to work was a relief, a welcome break. But slowly, over time, workdays and non-workdays merged. I began to feel sadness at work, flooded at inappropriate and apparently random times.

During one late afternoon class, I was lecturing on the idea of Health at Every Size. "We often inappropriately conflate weight and health," I explained, "and just because a person isn't fat doesn't mean that they are healthy . . ." My voice trailed off. Involuntarily, I recalled standing in a hospital room three years earlier, nurses marveling at my husband's trim body. "You don't look like a cardiac patient," they had told him. This memory flooded my eyes with tears. I froze.

Forty pairs of eyes looked at me. Some expressed confusion; some expressed concern. Still frozen, I considered leaving the room. Time passed. I wanted to resume the lecture but didn't know how to recover from this moment. Ultimately, I was honest about what had happened, about how my memory had taken over, how that had felt. Fortunately, the students seemed patient and receptive. This specific memory was a compelling example of the larger point. And yet, I felt I was losing control. Losing control of my voice, my composure, signaled a new chink in my shiny work armor.

The chink deepened with time. As months passed and winter broke, the shock of my husband's death sank deeper into my brain, under my flesh, penetrating my broken heart. As this happened, I showed more and more outward signs of distress. I cried even when alone, heaving loudly. The pain in my chest was near constant. Eyes burning, I read materials for work. Thighs screaming, I pedaled faster on the stationary bike. Tense and alone, I would lie in bed unable to sleep. I would not take sleeping pills. I would not drink alcohol. I would not be numb, caught unaware.

The semester ended, and it was a new calendar year. My chest literally ached all the time. Sometimes I couldn't even pretend to be okay. I stopped eating, filling myself with scalding hot herbal tea. I bought new clothing, in smaller sizes. People started to comment, complimentary rather than concerned. I began to wonder how little I could eat and still get away with it. Was I depressed? Was I developing anorexia? Was I trying to exert control over an uncontrollable world? Was I punishing myself? Was I unwilling to feed my hollowness, knowing that no food, no pills could fill my emptiness? Was I emulating my husband's new non-existence? Maybe. I don't know.

What I know is this: he was a body, then just a shell. And so was I.

Emptiness/Spaciousness

In early February, the candy and flowers displayed at the grocery store reminded me of how my late husband had once celebrated this day of love. With joy and pain, I recalled the first Valentine's Day after our marriage. On this day, Tris had surprised me with sapphire earrings in a stunning shade of light blue.

Over the course of a weekend, about six and a half months after Tris's death, many different factors retriggered my grief as I continued to learn to live a new life—alone.

A primary way loss ambushed me was as a single mother. Our teen daughter, Maddy, and I argued one Friday night. She asked me to drive her and her boyfriend to an early Valentine's Day dinner date on Saturday. I agreed. Then she asked me to drive her and a friend to breakfast on Sunday. I apologized but said, "No." Maddy's sense of injustice was excited. "Why not? They *always* drive and it's just not fair that we don't do our part." Something inside me gave way. Coldly calm, I pointed out the mathematical reality. Her other friends have two parents, which doubles the possible number of drivers. Maddy heard this but remained dissatisfied. I threw up my hands and went to our bedroom, a space that is now only my bedroom. I felt helpless, tearful, and unable to sleep.

The next afternoon, I found myself seated on a hard brown wooden pew in a sacred space. This was a moment when I really felt Tris's absence. He had never before missed one of Maddy's violin recitals.

We always sat together, touching hands, exchanging glances during the children's songs, the teacher's speech, the mingling afterward. When our girl played, Tris had beamed and recorded the moments on his high-tech camera equipment. Now Maddy has only half of her personal audience. My presence, no matter how attentive, can never fill the empty space next to me.

The music was beautiful. Continuously, I cried. Over and over, I'd breathe and wait for the wave of pain to build, peak, and dissolve, leaving only emptiness behind. Her technique was exquisite. She had made tremendous progress as a musician since the last recital; she had started with a new instructor just a couple of weeks before Tris's sudden death. I felt both amazed and heartbroken for her as well as for him, each missing the other.

On Sunday, I went to yoga. Before class began, the teacher spread essential oils on our wrists. Lemon and lavender deliciously comingled. Involuntarily, the scent evoked memories of a special vacation spot where Tris and I spent many of my birthdays. These memories of the past led me to think of the future. The two of us will never be there together again. We will never be together again, anywhere, in any space. I started to cry. I cried and I breathed, waiting for the wave of pain to build, peak, and dissolve.

Our teacher began class by linking yoga to his day job, briefly describing the challenges of showing constant and unconditional love to rowdy eighth-grade students. "That's the practice," he said with a rueful shrug. He invited us to direct this same approach to ourselves. He suggested that we notice and reflect on our own inner struggles and align ourselves with spaciousness. Spaciousness can allow us to feel and authentically respond to struggle.

Join the space, not the struggle.

He advised that we approach difficult sensations with compassion and kindness. This advice touched me. After Tris died, there was so much empty space in my life—and my impossible task was to align with it. After class, I impulsively approached the teacher. Seated in front of him, head bowed low, I whispered that I was grieving and that he was helping me heal. I clasped his hand. He asked if he might hug me. His voice and arms were gentle. The pain built, peaked. I choked back a sob.

In the late afternoon, I visited a local art museum with a friend. We viewed paintings and sculptures. The last time I was at this museum was with Tris for an exhibit featuring Escher. Escher's work had felt surreal. I'd been disoriented by the shifting perspectives and never-ending impossible stairs and ramps. Now I looked back with a new perspective. In hindsight, this art forecasted my experience of grief. Like the humanoid figures in Escher's creations, I'm continuously rising and lowering through what feels like a never-ending, impossible maze.

A Letter to Grief

Dear Grief,

It's almost seven months now. I don't know what to say. You hurt me. At times, the pain is unbearable. I knew that you'd be awful—but I had no idea what experiencing you'd actually feel like. Truly, ignorance was bliss.

You are everywhere, inescapable. Sometimes I'm so sick of you that I wonder if I can stand another minute. I just can't take it. I need a break, an escape, an exit. But that's impossible.

You're a relentless ghost, haunting me no matter where or when I happen to be. Sly and slimy, you've coiled tightly around me. You constrict my breath, my body, my spirit. You're a stone-cold concrete anchor wedged into my heart, a weight pulling me down hard and heavy into the depths of watery despair. A malignant virus, you've entered my body and overwhelmed my system by festering and multiplying. You fog up my brain. You strain my heart. You roil my gut.

Once I shared my life with my husband. Now, grudgingly, I share my life with you. You're my cruel new intimate companion. I'm a hostage, a prisoner. You stole me away from my happy life; like a captured child bride, I had no say. Helpless to stop you, I'm forced to bow to your will, to submit to your demands.

You bristle, feeling unjustly accused. You whisper, softly, that you're not a villain, not a captor. You're just part of death and, so, you're just part of life. You say that you're here to guide me, to help me, to shape me into a more compassionate person. You say that, thanks to you, I can better appreciate the joys of life in contrast to the bitterness of loss. After all, the great pain is simply the price of great love. You remind me that, because you're everywhere, I never have to feel alone. Dark and hooded, skeletal arms extended, you beckon me to accept you, appreciate you, embrace you.

I do not. Like the child I now seem to be, I want to kick and scream. This is so unfair. *No. No. No.* You ask too much. You ask for more than I can give.

For now, I resist. But at some point, I'll have to start to accept you. I'll need to find a way, although I have no idea how that will happen or what that will look like. What I do know is that—against my wishes—you've pervaded my life, my body, and my spirit. You're everywhere. And, like it or not, you're now a part of me. Like it or not, when I hate you, I also hate myself.

J

Viability

Dearest Tris,

In a couple of weeks, it'll be nine months since your death. Nine months feels like a significant marker. Culturally, nine months is tied to pregnancy. Eight and a half months in, my grief is now the size of a pumpkin—or maybe a small watermelon.

During pregnancy, a new potential person grows and develops. It takes time for webbing to spread into fingers and for eyes to shift to the front of the face. It takes time to develop functional lungs and a skeletal structure of bones. Beyond time, luck also is needed. The lucky potential person develops from sturdy materials, no missing or extra chromosomes. The lucky potential person exists in a hospitable environment, free from infection or invasive tests, with access to adequate nutrition. The lucky potential person is fully and completely cherished.

After a death, there's a different type of rebirth for those who are left behind. A new potential person grows and develops, despite having lost a critical part of the most vital organ of all: the heart. It takes time for the dented left ring finger to smooth out and for tears to stop uncontrollably leaking. It takes time for the mental fog to lift, for full breaths to replace shallow heaves, for trust to develop that one's own skeletal structure can stay upright. Luck also is needed. One is lucky to have emotional support and casseroles baked with heaps of love. One is lucky to have been fully and completely cherished by the person who is now gone.

I was incredibly lucky to have had you, to have been your wife.

In pregnancy, the age of viability is about seven months. This is the stage at which one is vulnerable but could probably survive. I'm now past this stage. I will probably survive. I've been living independently from the marital nest, the symbolic womb. Apparently, I have the ability to grow and develop on my own.

Losing you has allowed me to be reconfigured, to be reshaped, to gestate into a new form—to remain permanently incomplete, yet ever-evolving.

Your Jenny

Almost Normal

About sixteen months after losing my husband, I'm living an almost normal life. I go to work, to the gym, to the store. I see friends and visit family. I read and write. I make plans, at times looking forward with hope.

For a long time after Tris died, it felt like nothing really mattered. But some things have started to feel like they matter now. The pain is still here, always, but it's buried several layers deep. It's like a thin, porous layer of emotional scar tissue has grown around my heart. The pain bubbles up and out after peaceful moments: toward the end of a solitary walk, a yoga class, or a quiet massage. The pain also rises on specific occasions, during grief counseling, or on milestones and holidays—times when he should be here.

Some changes in my almost normal life are hard to take. In the months immediately after Tris died, most people acted kindly, with compassion. Some people have now changed. As their sympathy has faded, so has their kindness. They've stopped cutting me slack. Those who had been reluctant to ask for special favors or special treatment no longer show this reticence. They no longer worry about imposing. Maybe they've forgotten. And as time has passed, I keep meeting new people, new students, new colleagues. As I develop new connections, more and more I find myself interacting with people who have no idea that my world completely collapsed. At times, people who forgot and people who never knew make unreasonable demands. Inside, I whisper: *But my husband died!* Outside, I say, "Sorry. I'd love to but can't."

In the hallways at the high school orchestra concert, I run into other parents of other teens. I see these acquaintances look at me, curious, wondering why I'm alone, wondering where Tris is. Then I see them remember, which makes them look at me again, with pity.

I exercise every day, walking on a steeply inclined treadmill for an hour. It's compulsive. If I skip a day, I feel desperately out of control. With exercise, I can control my weight, my health, my mood. I exert this control. It looks almost normal. But it's not.

Other changes feel more positive. Now that more time has passed, most of my relationships are less one-sided. In general, I'm giving support just as much as I receive it. And I've told enough people enough times that disclosing the facts no longer makes me flinch: "My husband is dead. I'm a single parent. Yes, I was married, but now I'm a widow. "

I watch people get overwhelmed by deadlines, delays, and daily hassles. I sympathize despite an overall sense of detachment, remembering how it felt to be stressed like that. Loss has offered me a broader perspective. There's always something to be thankful for, always some kind of upside. I find and focus on the positive aspects of situations. Conflict offers clarity about where we each stand, what's needed to move forward, whether moving forward is worth it. Loneliness offers solitude.

These days, it's harder to take slights personally. I can see that other people's complaints are more about them than me. There are reasons why they want what they want, why they're frustrated or why they misbehave. I observe their disapprovals with calmness. I don't judge my critics for their desires, goals, or frustrations. Also, I'm not obligated to take action, to mollify, or to soothe them.

I'm more patient, more present. Unlike before, I pause, pondering options. I'm much less likely to jump into taking action. An internal compass guides me: *Slow down. No matter what, you'll get there.*

These days, I can look at the days and months ahead without being completely overwhelmed with the sadness of knowing that Tris will still be gone. It's still incredibly sad. But it's no longer incredible. It's how the world is now. There's nothing to be done but to look for peace.

I feel and express love intensely, holding nothing back. These days, I tell my children, my family, and my friends how much they mean to me: "I can't wait to see you. I adore you. You are everything." It is truth.

REFLECTING ON PAIN

- If you could go back and control what happened on the day you lost someone you loved, what would you want to have happen? Why? How might those changes affect your feelings now?

- In what ways does life after loss seem surreal? How do you ground yourself at those times?

- Does your loved one visit you in dreams? What does this feel like? How does the prospect of dreaming affect your sleep behaviors?

- People who are grieving often experience anger. At what times do you find yourself feeling angry at others? At yourself?

- When do you notice yourself feeling empty and in what ways?

- How do you take care of yourself when you feel overwhelmed with the pain of grief? What helps you manage those moments? Who in your life allows you to feel the pain without offering you quick fixes, rushing you through it, or downplaying its importance?

PART II
Expanding in Love

Since his passing, my social interactions have been shaped by longing for my beloved husband. In grief, I've also connected to a fuller range of intense emotions marked by conflict and contradiction. Celebrations and joyful moments are bittersweet because he can't share them with us. Powerful feelings of sadness and yearning reflect back the depth of love we once shared.

The essays in this section describe how I found different ways to connect to my own inner experience as well as with other people. Some describe relationships forged with new acquaintances, including psychic mediums and other widows. Others describe different ways of relating to family and friends, both old and new.

Valentine's Day

This is my first Valentine's Day as a widow. My husband, Tris, died just over six months ago.

Earlier in my life, Valentine's Day was a bad day. Tris knew this. Still, he remained optimistic that he could turn my head, change my mind. He tried to find ways to make me enjoy this designated day of adoration. For him, Valentine's Day was an opportunity to express his boundless love. For me, this day had different, darker meanings.

Tris's approach to Valentine's Day mirrored his general approach to our relationship. He was thoughtful and generous. On an early dinner date, when he realized my habit of ordering the least expensive menu entrée, Tris set himself on a mission to "spoil me" with love. And he did. Whenever he encountered something he thought I'd enjoy, he'd splurge, always eager to see my eyes shine. Even on random occasions, he continuously brought me books and baubles, cards and candy, trinkets and tickets. Every week, when he shopped for groceries and planned meals, he also bought me a bouquet of fresh flowers. Every holiday and anniversary, he offered the perfect card and gift. On my twenty-nineth birthday, we flew to San Francisco. He bought me yellow gold and white diamond earrings, which he casually left for me to find on an airplane seat. I was charmed and thrilled. It was then *more* surprising to find a second pair of beautiful earrings awaiting me on a connecting flight.

This quiet man—with his full, generous heart—couldn't have been a better valentine. He surprised me with luxury. He documented our adventures and made annual photo albums so we could savor our past memories together. As my valentine, his motives were simple and pure, as was his love for me and our children. I appreciated him and his efforts. I loved him dearly. And yet, each Valentine's Day, I remained skeptical, reluctant to fully embrace his romantic gestures.

Before I married Tris, Valentine's Day was difficult.

When I was a child, my father would buy me extravagant Valentine's gifts. In my memory, as a six-year-old, I received bouquets of blood-red roses secretly left by my bed for me to discover upon waking. Dad also bought me boxes of chocolate-covered cherries, so viscous and sickly sweet as to make the stomach ache. I was his very special girl, his beautiful princess—me and only me. In my memory, no one else received similar gifts: not my brother, sister, or mother.

When I was a teen, Dad would take me out to dinner or concerts. Once, we traveled together to Barbados. On these occasions, because of the particular type of affection he had for me, others often assumed that I was his much younger girlfriend.

Throughout my adolescence, Dad continued to play an important role in my experiences of Valentine's Day. When I was fifteen years old, my very first boyfriend cooked me a special Valentine's Day dinner. He hung tiny white lights on the ceiling and lit candles on the table. After dinner, these lights darkened. While a movie played on the TV, he kissed me deeply, passionately. I was dizzy with desire and pleasure. Suddenly, later, my heart and world flipped. Back in my family's driveway, as I was exiting this boyfriend's car, Dad was exiting the front door of our home, suitcase in hand. "What's happening?" I asked. Tersely, Dad said, "I just can't do this anymore." Then he drove away. My mother, inside, was hysterical. Their marriage had ended.

Two years later, on February 13, my stomach hurt. This time I was dizzy with fever. Dad had moved out. Mom was working nights and sleeping days at her boyfriend's apartment. Most of the time, we were unsupervised. My brother threw keg parties. My boyfriend slept over on the weekends. Late on the eve of Valentine's Day, a school night, I called my boyfriend's mother, crying and complaining of intense stomach pain. In my memory, she called Mom, who took me to the hospital. My appendix was removed on February 14. My once-absent father reappeared, bringing expansive bunches of blood-red roses left by my bed for me to discover upon waking. He also brought roses for the nurses. They marveled at his apparently unmatched devotion to his adolescent daughter. "You're so lucky," they told me.

This was false, of course. But later it ended up being true. As an adult, I was incredibly lucky to marry Tris and to build a life with him. We had a happy relationship and family. He left me with almost no regrets.

But I do regret my behavior on our past Valentine's Days. Despite his many efforts, his creativity, his generosity—in general and, specifically, on this day—I rejected this romantic holiday. I joked that Valentine's Day should be referred to as VD, like venereal disease, because both leave many people dissatisfied with their love lives. I complained about how this fake, capitalist holiday feels like a conspiracy designed to guilt people into spending money to perform superficial acts of love. I lectured on how Valentine's Day wraps misogyny in itchy lace and calls it romance.

I was defiant, oppositional. I did not graciously receive all that Tris generously offered. I loved him, passionately and completely, but rejected this holiday and his efforts on its behalf. How easy would it have been to simply soften? Yet, I stood firm. And now he's gone.

I have another, related regret: when our daughter was a toddler, Tris told me that he had bought her a Valentine's Day card. I received this news poorly. Fierce and angry, I told him, in no uncertain terms, that he could *not* give our daughter a card. "How inappropriate," I scolded. "This is a holiday for lovers—*not* for fathers and daughters."

His eyes went sad. "Okay," he said, "but it's really cute. See, look, here's Snoopy." My heart melted.

If he was here today, I'd apologize with my whole heart. I'd tell him that he did, in fact, succeed in his mission. I've truly been spoiled. He gave me a great love, every day, including on this designated annual holiday. What wouldn't I give to have him here again, just one more time, to join him in his silly, thoughtful gestures without a single complaint or raised eyebrow? I'd tell him that I now understand something new about Valentine's Day: it's a day of love—*not* only for lovers.

Although it's too little, too late, now I try to honor him on Valentine's Day. I embrace this day as a time to express love to important people. All of these friends remind me, time and again, how lucky I still am. They remind me of how much love there still is in this world.

After Tris's unexpected death, my friend Beth was the first person I called for help. Although she must've been completely stunned, she responded immediately, "I'll be right there." And she was. She was soft, holding me, and equally strong, keeping me upright. She made phone calls and took notes. She made lists of things I might need. She gently redirected me away from tasks such as driving to the airport to pick up visitors. In the very darkest hours, she made sure that I wasn't alone. More than six months later, she still checks in with me at least every other day. I bask in her unconditional love and unflagging support. When I'm unsure about how I feel or what to do, which is often, I call Beth. She's my anchor. I love her.

My friend Ellen was traveling when she heard the news of Tris's sudden death. She immediately abandoned her vacation plans and turned around for home. Steady and clear-eyed, she accompanied me and my stepson to the hospital to see his father's body and to the funeral home to help us plan the service. She advocated for our family when the hospital misplaced Tris's body and when the minister dismissed my request for a secular ceremony. She praised my children and me for coming together without tension or conflict. Ellen also opened her home to visitors, hosting our extended family overnight. Now, when I doubt my interactions with others or when I develop new, embarrassing medical symptoms, I call Ellen for advice. I love her.

My friend Silvia was already on vacation when Tris died. She returned as soon as she could but regularly called to check in, helpless with distance. Upon returning home, she worked with Ellen to order catering; she also arranged for string musicians to play at the funeral. She paid them directly, having ripped up my check. Regularly, in the months after the funeral, we had dinner together. During these meals, Silvia directly coached me about asking for help. "We are here," she said, firmly and repeatedly. "Call on us, please." She also coached me on turning down requests from people who don't seem to know or care that I'm a new widow and single mom: "Tell them that you'd love to, and you can't. Don't say more than that." It's been magical advice. When I need someone to drive my daughter or to join me for a lonely evening, I call Silvia. I love her.

Our friends, Karen and Dan, invite Maddy and me for a weekly "family dinner." They cook delicious meals. They listen patiently to my questions about lawn care and disposing of old paint cans. We discuss the challenges of parenting a teen. They offer help. They recommend books and movies. They introduced me to Camp Widow and offered to host my daughter when I went. Without hesitation, they agreed to become Maddy's custodial guardians should I die unexpectedly. When I need laughter or advice on domestic matters, I call Karen and Dan. I love them.

A friend/colleague at work, Jim, lost his young daughter in a tragic accident the year before Tris died. This heartbroken man generously spends time with me on a regular basis. Periodically, we drink coffee together before our first classes of the day. He asks how I'm doing.

When I share updates, he tells me that Tris would be proud of me. I'm overcome with gratitude to share space with him. I'm overcome with gratitude to hear him use Tris's name. Interacting with this man—who is kind, gentle, and brilliant in ways which remind me of my beloved—is the closest experience I have to interacting with Tris himself. Also, Jim is uniquely attuned to my grief in ways even Tris probably couldn't be. I love him.

And there are so many others. I'm surrounded by love, even on the saddest of Valentine's Days.

The Medium Place

About six and a half months after my husband died, a friend unexpectedly invited me to a free "meditation class" conducted by a psychic medium. My friend described what to expect: First, the medium would offer an informal lecture focused on spiritual but not religious insights. Next, at some point, she'd talk about the spirits who "came through" for those of us in the room. Finally, at the end, there would be guided meditation. He described the medium as kind and respectful to all, believers and non-believers alike. I appreciated this openness.

My friend said that he had attended this class after his father died a few years ago. He told me that the medium had known things she couldn't possibly have known without connecting to his father's spirit. This friend described his experience as interesting and healing. He also said he wanted me to have the same opportunity to reconnect with Tris. Touched by his empathy, I also felt intrigued by how positively he described his own experience.

I'd never before considered consulting with a psychic medium. The first time the possibility had even entered my consciousness was during a religious grief support group. My experience of this group was wildly uneven; it was sometimes helpful, sometimes horrible. One horrible meeting focused on a discussion of heaven and the afterlife. During this meeting, facilitators warned us against participating in séances or similar attempts to contact our loved ones. These are my notes from their presentation:

You may be tempted to see a medium. The Bible warns against this. It is detestable to the Lord to use sorcery or fortune telling. An understandable impulse but do not be tempted. Look to God for answers. If too focused on our lost loved one, we miss out on how God can take care of us. Widow says it's facing reality to talk to God but not to her dead spouse! An undistracted focus on the Lord is an opportunity to honor God by building a relationship with Him, by discussing things in our lives. Nothing is too small to bother God about, including the house and lawn care.

After paraphrasing the presentation into these choppy partial sentences, I remember looking around the room at the other bereaved group members. There were many crumpled, dejected faces. Clearly, some bereaved people here had already tried to connect with their lost loved ones. A flash of anger jolted through me. Why criticize them for this? Why label attempts to reconnect as sinful? These people were in profound pain. And so, why not allow them—allow *us*—to do whatever we can to find a sense of connection, comfort, or peace? Partly in rebellious response to this specific memory, I agreed to attend the medium's class. I was glad to have the chance to defy the facilitators' stern prohibitions.

While driving to the meditation class, I felt a mix of emotions. I was excited yet skeptical, hopeful yet worried about being hopeful. Was attending this class stupid and self-defeating? My desire to reconnect with Tris was overwhelming. Wasn't that, at least partly, because such a reconnection is impossible? I tried to make myself stay open to the experience, regardless of whether Tris's spirit "came through." At the same time, being "open" also seemed like being "vulnerable" to deception or manipulation.

Tris was a staunch non-believer. Like me, he had one parent who was Jewish and one who was not. He rejected organized religion but joined the local Unitarian Church so that our children would have access to religious education. Unlike me, he also rejected spirituality within even mainstream practices such as reflexology and yoga. There was absolutely no way he would ever consult with a person who claimed to have psychic gifts—for any reason, under any circumstances. I was less sure, a muted agnostic in the shadow of his vivid atheism.

My friend and I arrived at the two-hour class almost a full hour before it was scheduled to begin. Many rows of seats, mostly white plastic chairs, faced the front of the room. A relaxed looking man seated near the door greeted us as we entered. Various diplomas and certificates hung on a bone-white wall in front of the chairs. The other walls of the room blushed a subdued peach-pink hue. We were surrounded by eclectic art and inspirational sayings. An invitation to "believe, love, breathe" hung on the wall near a dangling dream catcher adorned with turquoise beads and feathers.

We had our choice of where to sit. My friend suggested that the floral couch in the room's center would be the most comfortable option. Others trickled in, gradually filling the white plastic chairs all around us. Voices were hushed like in church. Some people seemed to know one another, to happily reunite. Some voices became louder, laughing. A prayer sheet was passed around so that we could make a written request for prayers on behalf of our loved ones.

The medium entered the room at 7:00 p.m. sharp. She was casually dressed in a pink knit sweater and dark framed glasses. She looked like a middle-aged neighbor who might visit on Sunday afternoon to share a loaf of banana bread or an apple pie. Her voice was both loud and gentle. She told meaningful and often humorous stories about relatives she'd lost through death and memories she keeps from their time together. She talked about her part Italian, part Native American cultural and familial heritage. She occasionally cursed, with comic effect. She punctuated her speech with phrases meant to connect her words to our thoughts: "Do you know?" "Isn't that right?" and "Do you know what I mean?" She called each of us "honey."

Then the medium counseled us as to the importance of being open to the gift of life and the wisdom we all carry within ourselves. She spoke about that night's full moon connecting us to our own hearts and to one another, to those on this earth and to those spirits (or angels or guardians or whatever the word is for the forces) guiding us from other realms. She advised us to identify our inner thoughts as ideas created and affected by our families and our cultures, by programming and conditioning. She invited us to differentiate these inner thoughts from our sense of inner wisdom. Wisdom, she said, is Truth that we both know and feel. Wisdom is within our hearts and is an essential part of all that really matters, which is Love.

These opening words struck me as profound. Tears pricked at my eyes. What she said felt absolutely true. What she said described my new way of existing in the world, a new way forged through the pain of Tris's death. There is only Love. But at the same time, what the medium said also felt like *exactly* what someone would say to prime us to look for convergence, corroboration, confirmation. With this thought, I sat up straighter—more alert, spine erect.

The medium continued talking, telling stories, offering guidance. Then she began making observations about apparent spirits in the room, "Someone is here for you. Who is Mike? Or Michael? Is he your brother? Cousin? Oh, he is funny. He is joking around. He wants to hug you. His arms are around you right now. Oh, honey, he's looking more serious. He wants you to know that he is sorry. He did his best. He knows he could've done better, and he wishes he did, but he loves you. Know that. Remember that, honey. He's going to come visit you in your dreamscape. You know that's when they approach you, sometimes, in your dreams."

Systematically, she moved from the front to the back of the room, addressing some people in each row but not each person. She relayed silent conversations that she had with different spirits and described seeing different spiritual forms. Some were individual adults: a husband, a grandmother, a sister. She also described seeing an unborn child lost through miscarriage and a trio of friends, all of whom had passed. At one point, she described seeing the spirit of a beautiful white horse.

When she spoke to people directly in front of me, my breath quickened. I filled with anxious hope. My gut roiled with turmoil as my heart lifted with promise. I felt moved. I felt skeptical. I longed for her to connect me to Tris. I was terrified that she would connect me to Tris.

What if it was wonderful? What if it was terrible? What if, either way, I fell completely apart?

At some point, the medium directed her attention to my friend. She expressed enthusiastic compliments about his extraordinary aura, his energy. As she marveled over his apparently abundant spiritual gifts, he squirmed. My friend seemed both pleased and uneasy to be publicly praised as some kind of spiritual Adonis. Both his pleasure and uneasiness were contagious. I felt flattered to be seated next to him, illuminated by his glorious aura. Although I didn't fully understand the compliments she offered, nothing sounded incorrect. My friend is a warm, kind person. Then I caught myself wondering if this was some kind of deliberate set up. Had he invited me here to witness this effusive performance? Immediately, I dismissed this idea as unfairly paranoid and tried to let it go.

The medium then said something along the lines of, "There's a man behind you. He's holding onto his chest. I can't tell. Did he have a heart attack? Or maybe he is heartbroken? I asked him if he had a heart attack, but he just said, 'I had a heart problem—a problem with my heart.' I'm not sure. Is this your dad?" My friend responded, "Possibly, yes." His father had died several years ago. He may have had heart problems. The medium told him that the man wanted my friend to know "this won't happen to you." Also, there was some kind of paperwork in an envelope, maybe a contract. It should be read very carefully. The medium then asked about someone named Richard, maybe Dick. My friend responded that he was unsure whether his father knew anyone with either name.

At this point, the medium seemed to regard the two of us together, as a pair or a unit. She said something that made it seem like she assumed we were colleagues with the same employer. But this was incorrect. Then, attending directly to me (*finally!! at last!!*), she asked where I worked. I vaguely responded, "At a college." She said that someone had died there recently, within the past three or so months. She said it was "medical, a virus of some sort," and the person was "young or perhaps 40." I shrugged, wordless, remembering that a young undergraduate student in our department had tragically died last week. I didn't know how or why. In fact, we had never met. Was there another death—someone who I knew, who might be more inclined to "come through" in this place on this evening? Silent, I felt confused and guilty, as if I was being uncooperative and ungrateful. The medium moved on, redirecting her attention to others, leaving me disappointed and also strangely relieved.

After the guided meditation, the class ended. My friend and I talked about what the medium had said to us. He told me that the medium had been confused. He pointed out that we were seated next to one another. A man who appeared behind him, he said, also appeared behind me. This possibility felt shocking. "It was Tris," my friend said. This wasn't an idea that I had considered: "But, so, then . . . was that really for you? Or for me? And is the contract in the envelope something that I should read carefully? And am I supposed to be the one who knows Richard, or Dick?"

That evening, my default response was disagreement. But over the next several days, I began to consider the possibility that Tris had "come through" based on three aspects of the medium's description. First, according to the chart notes, the last thing that Tris had done was to clutch his chest while garbling unintelligibly. He remained alive but also in an altered mental state upon arriving at the hospital. His heart seized up and stopped beating almost as soon as he was wheeled into the cardiac unit. The chest-clutching description fit. Second, Tris was certainly heartbroken to leave our children, to leave me. Also, he had died of a sudden heart attack. Both interpretations seemed simultaneously true. Both fit.

The third element was more subtle. The medium had reported that the "spirit" did not/would not directly answer her question about why he was clutching his chest. Similarly, Tris had a mischievous tendency to remain mysterious—to teasingly refuse answers to my questions. There were countless examples of this pattern:

"Where are we going for dinner?" I'd ask. "Although I love you without reservations," he'd say, "we have reservations at 6:00 p.m. at an undisclosed location."

"How could you possibly know that obscure bit of information?" I'd wonder aloud. "Because I know all," he'd teasingly respond.

"Do you think [insert name of random celebrity] is attractive?" I queried as we watched a film. "Jenny's attractive." he'd reply. "Yes, yes, but what about *her*?" I'd press. He'd smile, repeating, "Beautiful Jenny. Jenny is beautiful."

"Why are you doing that? What's going on?" I would ask. "Because I love you," he'd reply.

Perhaps fittingly, my first psychic experience left me with many questions without answers. Days later, I struggled to find a place of balance within myself. Months later, I still struggle to find a way to integrate vastly discrepant thoughts and feelings about truth and faith, about reality and meaning, about life and death.

The Medium

Almost seven months after my husband died, I met with another psychic medium. Typing these words makes me cringe. But it's the truth. Not everything this medium said seemed to make sense or to fit, but some of her comments did. The time absolutely flew by. I would've said we talked for ten minutes, not sixty.

At about 1:00 p.m. on a cold day in late February, I arrived at the office of this psychic medium. She was an attractive woman wearing tasteful jewelry. She greeted me with a smile and a handshake, flinching slightly after feeling my icy hand. The medium took my coat and invited me into a small dark room. She asked me to sit on a chair with a soft red pillow resting on it. To the right of my chair was a small table with a box of tissues, carefully placed. She sat directly across from me. To her left, on a low table, audio equipment recorded our session. She set a timer for one hour and then began.

First, she explained what I could expect and how this worked. She told me that, as an empath, she could feel things within her body which she would relay to me. She would call on spirits to join us. It was up to me to tell her who I wanted to hear from; she wouldn't provide information from any spirits without my permission. She told me that she wouldn't tell me anything that would make me paranoid, nor would she predict my death or the death of others. She said that she believed in free will and human choice. If she forecasted something that might happen, I could decide if I wanted to make choices to either match that outcome or deviate from it. The medium also told me that she would be interpreting information and would need time and space to communicate with the spirits internally before she could share the interpretation. She indicated that she would ask me if what she said made sense, even if it didn't fully make sense to her. She said that sometimes she heard words and sometimes spirits showed her images or positioned themselves in postures that she could then interpret.

I started to tear up. My breath quickened. I felt intensely vulnerable. What was about to happen? What would she tell me? Would this be healing, harmful—both? Would I regret this choice? The medium observed my wet eyes and told me that it was okay for me to have strong feelings. I appreciated her validation. Still, it was hard to make eye contact.

The medium began by holding both of my hands in her own. Her skin was warm, and her touch was gentle. She opened with a prayer, reverent, asking for spirits to come to us "through the white light of God." She held my hands for a few minutes, then released them. She said she wanted to tell me what she felt. She told me that my left hand represented my competencies, my abilities to advocate for myself and others, motion and movement. She said she felt some blockage, as if there were rocks in our hands. She told me that my right hand represented my emotions and that she could feel them whirling about, spinning. It was chaos, she said. Then she observed that these two sides of myself were in turmoil, mixed up together. She said it felt like grief. I nodded, feeling impatient. *Of course, it was grief!* Why else do people set up meetings with psychics?

After a pause, the medium said that she felt the spirits of several people: man, man, woman, woman, man, woman, man. She said most were not related to me. Irrationally, I began to worry that Tris wouldn't come. Of course, he wouldn't participate in this. Although, anything was possible. Wasn't that why I was here?

The medium asked who I hoped to hear from, and I told her that my husband had died last August. She warmly expressed her condolences. She seemed to connect this new information to whatever energy she felt within my hands. She said that my husband seemed to be the first male spirit she sensed. She told me she'd tell me what he had to say and that I could ask him questions, if I wanted.

The medium began by saying she had the sense of tragedy. She said that he apologized, over and over. He was sorry. He was sorry to leave us. She said that his end of life was jumbled and uncertain, similar to a sense of swirling—like at the start of the old TV show, *Twilight Zone*. She said that there were sirens and the sound of wheels on pavement. He heard voices but from far away.

She expressed a feeling of discomfort about something the spirit said to her. He repeatedly used the word "responsible." She said she got the sense that he was a caring person who did what he felt was right. There may have been something he did, or something he didn't do, that he felt may have been related to his death. I nodded. She said that he wanted to reassure me that there was nothing I could do, no way to stop it. He told her to tell me he hadn't been waiting. I wondered if this was in reference to the text message he had sent me, the one I hadn't seen until it was too late.

She told me she continued to feel worried about the word "responsible." She hated to ask, but, "Did he die by suicide?" No, I assured her. She sighed, visibly relieved. She told me that he referred to me as "his partner, his friend; his partner, his friend." She said he repeated these words over and over. She said that we seemed to have a genuine connection, one that she was sorry to say that she doesn't always see. She said that his presence didn't seem to fit with the idea of suicide. He didn't want to leave us.

I wondered about this word: *responsible*. Tris was hyper-responsible, conscientious, and rule bound. He died directly after a workout with his personal trainer. He came home from the gym, short of breath and gray of face. He spoke on the phone with a colleague for about thirty minutes before searching the phrase "heart attack symptoms" on the internet. Then he called 911. Did he blame himself for a tough workout, for ignoring his symptoms until it was too late—or for something else?

She told me that he said the two of us had nothing left unsaid. There were no regrets. I sobbed. She said that he showed her a photo of the two of us, possibly from our wedding. She said that I was in a lacy dress and that he was so proud. She said he told her that this was the day that changed his life, that made his life complete. If he could come back and do it all over, he'd marry me again. I continued to sob, struggling for breath.

The medium spoke for a while before I ventured to ask: "At the end, was he afraid?" She paused, as if to consult, and then told me that the end of his life was similar to what is portrayed in a drowning scene on TV. The drowning person sees the light above while sinking into the dark. The darkness grows bigger and bigger until there's no more light, no more to see. "He is better now," she said. "He says he feels better. And he's no longer cold." She described that this last part didn't make sense to her because it had been summer. I didn't mention his blue-gray hands and feet, his poor circulation.

The medium told me that he showed her that we had two children, one boy and one girl. My heart lifted in surprise. How could she know this? She told me that my husband and I raised two good people. She said my husband was incredibly proud of our young man. He indicated this by standing up very straight. He said he could see that our son was sad but also smart, competent, and taking steps to move forward. She also said my husband was sorry to miss important events in our daughter's life. She said that she could see photos of him—a collage—in our daughter's room. (My eyebrows raised. Maddy has a wall covered in photos next to her bed.) The medium said that she could see that he had strong love for our daughter, that he would stroke her hair and gently kiss her forehead while she slept. I indicated that our daughter was turning sixteen in a few days. The medium nodded and said that this was an important milestone. The medium said my husband wanted us to know he was still "at the table," still with us. She said that our children "wear him" but she wasn't sure what that meant. Was it possible that one might want a commemorative tattoo? I shook my head vigorously. *No.* She apologized and said that wearing him might mean many different things, not just tattoos. I shrugged.

She told me that my husband wanted me to know that there was a future—a life forward—for all of us. There's more to enjoy. He wants us to move forward and will stay with us, always be with us. Even if we relocate to a different house, he'll be with us. Our house may be a burden. He wants me to do what I think is best. He is with me, not the house. He hears me talk to him. He sees me go to his closet, hold his clothes, talk to him. He hears me, and he responds with love. He wants to hug me, to give me a rose, to tell me that I'm not alone and that he is with me, as much as he can be. She says she can tell he was very romantic. I nodded, thinking of myself late at night, caressing his suit jackets and dress shirts, wondering whether it'll ever feel like the right time to clean out the closet.

The medium told me that he was a gentle man and also a gentleman. She could tell he was humble and civic-minded, thinking of others beyond himself. She told me that he sensed there was some kind of posthumous honor for him; he was grateful and also thought that it was an acknowledgment of both his work and his relationships, including coworkers and family. The medium said that she could feel that he and I had built a strong family together, perhaps unlike the family from my childhood. She also said that she could see our son spending time at our home. She asked if he lived with us, in the same house, and I said not anymore. She indicated that when our son came home, I felt more complete and more myself. She said Tris didn't want Jonah to take on his dad's role, exactly, but he was proud of how Jonah could be helpful and help our family move on. She also said that she could see three graduation caps for our daughter. She predicted Maddy would have a high school diploma and then two additional degrees from college and beyond.

The medium said that it seemed like before he passed away Tris was doing paperwork, concerned about documents—and possibly a will or insurance or other legal matters. There was important work that had not been finished, and he was concerned about this because it affected other people. I told her it was likely his research grant. He had been doing important work. It remained unfinished. He wasn't able to complete it.

The medium asked if I had other questions. There was just one. I asked about the last gift he had given me, a book written by a widow, Kate Braestrup: *Here if You Need Me.* I asked why he had bought me that book. She paused, appearing distracted. Then she said that it wasn't a premonition. Rather, it had been a coincidence. He waved his hands, she said, indicating no. He had just thought it was something that I would enjoy, so he had bought it.

Some of what the medium said didn't seem accurate. She asked about someone with a name starting with a "D." (In hindsight, maybe the executor of Tris's estate?) At the time, I shrugged. She said that Tris was reunited with his mother who stood near a man with military connections. I have no idea who this man might be. She also asked if I had a grandmother who died, because she saw a grandma with my face. This grandma was holding a white blanket, usually indicating miscarriage. She asked if I had ever miscarried or if my grandmother had. I told her not me but possibly my grandma. I didn't know. She told me my grandma was giving love to the unborn baby and to Tris. I found this difficult to imagine, because Tris and my grandmother barely knew one another. She told me Tris had the sense that his car was gone and that, while he liked his car, it wasn't super important to him. The fact that it was gone was okay. Although this permissiveness seemed plausible, it's hard to imagine that Tris would talk about his car in the few minutes he might have to communicate from beyond.

I have no idea what was happening in the room. Was I was somehow sending signals that she was reading? When I made the appointment, I used only my first name, Jennifer. I said only that my husband had died. With this general information, there seemed no way for her to find out more about me in advance. Still, she seemed to know a lot that would be impossible to know.

No matter what's true and what's not, my psychic reading was a deep dive into grief. I had the chance to at least consider the possibility of being reconnected to my beloved. Through the medium, I heard him say goodbye, I heard him say that he was sorry to leave us. And that he, like I, had left nothing important unsaid. For this opportunity, I'm beyond grateful.

Love Letter Number Two

My Beloved,

It's just over seven months now since you've been gone.

At times, I still can't believe it. It feels incredible that I'll never again be able to hold your hand or stroke your hair. I ache to touch you again, for you to touch me. I'm starving, ravenous to smell your scent, to breathe your breath. Instead, I stand in front of your open closet and stroke the dress shirts that had touched the once warm skin over your once beating heart.

Although I miss your body—the smell and touch and feel of you—I also miss your mind, your wisdom, your clarity. You had such a broad perspective on our lives and the world around us. I miss your personality, your shyness, your sturdiness, and your silly puns. You appreciated the absurd. You taught me to find and to laugh at the funny parts of bad behavior and bad situations. I miss your generosity, how you'd buy me tulips and bring me treats. You'd ask about my day and listen patiently to my complaints, my worries, nodding and softly stroking my hand, my cheek. I miss your companionship, you seated next to me, talking about parenting or planning our next vacation. With you, the future was a fun and exciting place. I miss being yours, how proud I felt to be your life companion. I loved being the wife of the kind, brilliant scientist who worked tirelessly to make a difference in this world. I miss your flaws. You were often indecisive, flustered, forgetful. You were always buying new nail clippers.

This morning I had the image of our life together as a tall building with clean white walls. Your death smashed into this structure like a wrecking ball, leaving a gaping hole and debris everywhere. Our life is now my life—broken, fragmented, such a mess. The damage is massive and overwhelming. Is it even possible to clean this up? *Should I even try?* The cavernous hole has left me bare, exposed. The winds hit me directly now. I shiver and feel vulnerable, unsafe. I also wonder about the foundation. Is there enough of a base here? Will all that is left suddenly collapse? How will I be able to find a way to exist in these jumbled ruins?

Only time will tell. But time is the villain of our story. We didn't have enough time. There is no more time to be together. Our time is over. The world keeps spinning, the sun keeps rising, the clock keeps ticking. Time advances. Carried forward by new days, I move unwillingly, powerlessly, away from time with you.

Slowly and painfully, I'm adjusting. It's happening automatically, against my will. As the days pass, as I continue to live and you continue to be gone, your absence feels more and more familiar. The circular indent from our wedding band on my left ring finger, now naked, has been mostly smoothed away. Last night, mindlessly, I parked my car in the middle of the garage we once shared. I hate this, of course. I still want to tell you the good news, still want to lie next to you at night. But now I find that, when positive events occur, the old immediate urge to tell you has faded away. And when I force myself upstairs, stumbling into our bed in the darkest night hour, it's now familiar to find unwrinkled sheets and your unused pillow, bare and cold.

Yours always, with love,

J

CAMP WIDOW, PART ONE
Alone, Together

I'm on my way to Florida to attend Camp Widow. It's been seven months and fifteen days. Much like the March air, the plane is cold. I'm in a window seat next to a friendly man in a business suit. After I'm served a cup of water, this man invites me to share his tray because my own tray hangs lopsided, one hinge busted.

Suddenly, the sky shifts from black to a dark blue. Above white clouds, a thin line of rose pink glows below accents of light peach. It's so breathtakingly beautiful that my throat aches. I'm struck by an unexpected thought: maybe, right now, we are close to heaven. "Hello, my love," I whisper silently.

Tears fill my eyes. When I fly, I feel forced to completely submit, surrender, let go. There's just nothing else to be done. It's not unlike the complete emotional surrender required to give up being a wife, a partner, a love. Three months after Tris died, our daughter and I flew to visit family for Thanksgiving. I sobbed throughout the entire turbulent flight home because, in a world without Tris, nowhere actually feels like home.

I don't remember ever being lonely before being widowed. Half-jokingly, to shield the harshness of truth, I recently told a friend that my husband had "ruined me." Early in life, my goal was to be free and untrapped by toxic relationships. But that was long ago. I'm no longer content merely to avoid aversive people. Having had more, I seek more.

I yearn for moments of genuine connection. Only after Tris died did I realize exactly how blessed I was to be bonded to him, linked directly to his heart. Blindly, I'd taken for granted the pleasures of physical and emotional closeness, of daily intimacy, of sharing stories of success or failure, of highs and lows, of the sweet and bitter. When something happened, I could tell him immediately or anticipate, with certainty, a later conversation. There was safety, and also wisdom. When I could talk to Tris, we made sense of life, together. With him, I understood. Now, without him, my understanding is limited. Now, without him, less matters. When I was married, things happened to me, big and small. And all of these mattered to him because I mattered to him. Now that I'm widowed, many things happen and many of them matter to me—and only me.

This isn't to say that I don't have love and support. I'm blessed with wonderful children, caring relatives, and many loving friends. Other people regularly offer me opportunities for intimacy, for sharing, for connection. They reach out with texts, emails, phone calls, and visits. They praise me as brave for tackling my grief by attending grief support groups or a conference like Camp Widow; they may not realize that, for me, standing still is even more terrifying than stumbling forward. They commend my dedication to work, to parenting, to writing. They praise my fledgling attempts to build a fuller life. They sense, correctly, that I'm bereft without Tris's attention, his support, his love.

I worry about burdening them. I worry about needing too much. When they reach out and squeeze my hand (literally) or squeeze my heart (metaphorically), I find myself almost overwhelmed. These days, connection feels like quickly eating too much cotton candy or cake icing. There's an acute sweetness—a thrill tinged with a vague, thrumming ache. I try to fully savor these moments. They don't come often enough. In these moments, because my need is ravenous, the aching sweetness is that much more intense.

Alone, I arrive in Tampa. The sun is bright. Squinting, I enter the luxurious hotel, admiring the vaulted ceilings and cool, circulating air. Each adult person I see, I silently wonder: *Are you a widow? Are you?* I scan my surroundings. When I approach the front desk, although it's several hours before official check-in time, I'm offered a room. The clerk asks if I'd prefer a king or two double beds. I blink, stammering, "It doesn't matter." She is kind, but I want to cry. Instead, I smile weakly.

After a short nap, I head to the registration table. Standing behind a woman who was recently widowed and who is crying too hard to speak, I feel both sympathy and impatience. *I know. Me, too.* Eventually, it's my turn. As I check in, I receive a name badge that also lists my home city and state along with a ribbon and small, colorful pins. The "6-12 months" ribbon signals how long ago my husband died. I receive a red heart pin on which to write his initial and a "first camp" pin along with a lanyard that is yellow, rather than blue, which also signifies my status as a newcomer.

Everyone is a widow (or widower—although the majority of attendees, possibly 80 percent, are women). Everyone is very nice, welcoming, smiling. Still, the idea of mingling with all of this personal information visible on my chest feels odd and uncomfortable, so I escape upstairs to my hotel room. When a teenager joins me in the elevator, I position myself so as to cover my name tag. Wearing the badge, exposing my widowhood and especially with such a conspicuous display of detail, feels like the exact opposite of what I've been trying to do: to live a normal life, whatever that even means.

Later, I return to the camp area. Everyone is widowed, still. And they're from all over the country. There are many younger women here, people like me. And there also are many older people. Some had been legally married, and some had not. Some had been happily coupled before widowhood, and some had not. Some had children, and some had not. Some have since remarried, or re-partnered, and some have not. Regardless, each had lost their person, their life partner.

We read each other's badges to connect and chat. "It's your first camp, too? What was your spouse's name?" An unexpected shift takes place. I feel myself relax, surrounded by my people, my tribe. It's comforting and, also, inspiring. Look how many of us there are! And, look: we're all still standing. Throughout the weekend, I'm intimately bonded with hundreds of strangers. We are alone, together. In this place, being a widow connects rather than isolates. We discussed ways of integrating the past, present, and future. Collectively, we honored the deep love we still feel despite the losses we've endured.

One of the gifts of Camp Widow is normalization. Another gift is celebration, celebrating the love that continues. We also celebrated the gifts of community and friendship, of humility and vulnerability. We celebrated how we've grown as people with broader perspectives on what matters, what's important. Grief has made us feel more empathic, more compassionate. We showed these qualities by reaching out, tenderly and often. "How are you doing? Be sure to take breaks, if you need them." As the wonderful comedian Kelley Lynn Shepherd said at the conference, "I love my widow tribe but would trade them all in a heartbeat—in a hot minute—for the chance to have my husband back." We all share this. We all share so much.

Being surrounded by other widows was like being immersed in a tub of warm water. The relaxation spread across me. I exhaled, enjoying the gentle heat on my skin. The relaxation moved into me. My muscles softened, loosened. There was a kind of peace.

I failed to fully recognize and appreciate this peacefulness until it evaporated. Entering the airport, heading for home, I looked around for the widows I now expected to see. But they weren't here. Or, if they were, I couldn't tell. My time to feel warm, intimate connection with strangers had ended, and this realization flooded me with both loss and gratitude. As I rejoined the wider world, I receded into my pitied, stigmatized identity as bereft and incomplete. But for a time, this same identity was shared, honored, celebrated.

My eyes filled with tears as I boarded the plane home from Camp Widow. The aircraft approached the horizon as the sun rose, once again, amid shades of blue, rose, and peach. I whispered silently, childishly, to Tris: "Look! Are you proud? I'm actually doing this. Can you believe it? You should see this. You should be here."

"You should be here" is a phrase I learned at camp. It is a profound truth. But he is not. So I carry him with me, in my heart and in my memory—always. We are together, although I am alone.

CAMP WIDOW, PART TWO
All the Feelings

Attending Camp Widow, a conference entirely populated by women and men who had lost their life partners, was powerful and provocative. During my weekend in Tampa, I was transformed by hearing others' stories and perspectives about loss and resilience. Their words inspired me to think differently about my own story, my own loss, my own resilience. Hearing how some widows had rebuilt their lives was immensely reassuring. It became clear that the as-of-yet-unwritten part of my story will never erase the past. It became clear, too, that my love for Tris will remain pure and eternal, untarnished and undiminished—no matter what the future holds or what happens next.

Camp Widow, for me, offered a compassionate space to reconcile contradictions and complexity. At camp, I was reminded of a phrase that I once read: *a paradox is a truth standing on its head to get our attention.* Paradox comes from two Greek words: *para* and *doksos*, together meaning "beyond the teaching" or "beyond the opinion." Having looked up this word, I'm struck by the preposition "beyond." In grief, we are beyond what is known; we are groundless. There is only uncertainty, ambiguity, and unanswerable questions. *What am I supposed to do now? How can I go on?*

To embrace a paradox is to live with the tension of apparent contradictory truths. It is to accept a complex reality. To embrace a paradox is to acknowledge different ways to conceive of experience.

Although these different conceptions may conflict or even cancel one another out, in embracing paradox we resist the pull to cancel or collapse into a simplistic, single dimension. To embrace a paradox requires us to reconcile seeming contradictions, honoring each. We acknowledge that there are simultaneous truths, and truths aren't "either/or." Rather, truths are "both/and."

Surrounded by this community of support, I encountered multiple simultaneous truths. Some paradoxes were specific to camp. For example, most of us had never met before. Yet, because of our shared status, everyone at the conference seemed intimately familiar. And, at the same time that my heart broke for the other campers, I was thrilled to meet them—especially other younger widows like me. We are not alone. Or, rather: we are alone, together.

Camp Widow launched with a welcoming presentation by its founder/director. Brimming with charisma and compassion, she shared her personal story of widowhood and her initial attempts to make this conference a reality. She poked fun at her own naiveté and inexperience in the early days of this work. She described how she had made huge mistakes in planning the first Camp Widow, and she also shared what she learned from these mistakes. Through determination and creativity—through sheer grit—she channeled her experience of isolation into building an organization that connected others. As she described her hopes for each of us to connect and find a sense of belonging, I felt both inspired and sad.

Next, I attended an orientation workshop for new widows. The presenter, a woman in her early thirties, spoke in a quietly commanding way. First, she articulated her own story of tragedy and introduced some of the other widowed presenters. Next, she offered insights about grief, normalizing the rollercoaster of emotions, the sleeplessness, and the foggy, forgetful widow brain. She shared simple, powerful advice. The first suggestion was to breathe. She asked us to each take three deep breaths, pausing long enough for us to breathe together. On the third exhale, my eyes filled with tears. She then reminded us to take one step at a time, to be gentle with ourselves, and to avoid "should" statements as judgments. She advised us to drink water, eat healthy food, sleep whenever the urge strikes, and get fresh air, even if it's cold.

The presenter shared how it was helpful for her to keep sunglasses with her so that she could recede into herself at difficult or tearful moments, erecting a barrier between her own internal experience and the external world. (Brilliant advice!) She advised us to cut back on activities, to say, "No." She encouraged us to remember that we should each grieve in our own way, that only we know what each of us needs. Finally, she urged us not to forget: *Love. Never. Dies.* For another moment, my eyes filled again. The presenter spoke with the authority and compassion of experience. I felt deeply grateful to have received her wisdom borne of sadness.

After orientation and lunch, I attended another workshop offered by the camp director: "You Should Be Here." Enraptured, I sat in the front row. She opened with a discussion about our feelings when we encounter new events and new experiences without our loved ones. She told us that this was a brand-new workshop that she had been inspired to develop after her daughter's wedding. She shared stories and also invited others to share their stories.

Throughout the session, I began to realize that there are potentially endless variations on this essential phrase. *You should be here.* Our loved ones miss out on getting to use new technological gadgets, like the latest iPhone. *You should see this!* They don't get to enjoy the latest *Star Wars* movie or season of the TV show we enjoyed watching together. *You won't believe what happens next!* They miss celebratory events and occasions: graduations, marriages, anniversaries, birthdays, births. *You'd be so happy, so proud.* They miss sad events, too: illnesses, divorces, other deaths. *You'd be hugging us right now.* They aren't available to talk about the things we used to talk about together: our friends, our finances, our futures. *Can you believe what's happening?*

The camp director advised that, in all of these situations, it's important to acknowledge this simple, counterfactual truth: *You. Should. Be. Here.* Our loved ones should be here, for us and also, for others. Yet? They are not. She recommended that we acknowledge these truths by reaching out to others who also grieve the loss of our person. When we talk about our lost loved ones, we bring them into the present. And when we talk about our lost loved ones with others who also miss them, we offer opportunities for others to give and receive support. She suggested that just a brief phone call, even two minutes, can suffice. These brief moments of connection accumulate and build. These brief moments matter.

The camp director cautioned that, although we might feel that reaching out could seem like a burden, just one more thing to manage, reaching out to express our shared loss helps all of us heal. The loss is permanent and unchangeable, yet imagining what our person would do or say at important moments brings our person back to us, linking the past and the present. She said that we can honor our loved ones by acting on their behalf, by buying the birthday cards that they would have given us. We can honor them by including them, by leaving room for them at the holiday dinner table and by filling their Christmas stockings. She also invited us to consider how special it is to be the person who gets to introduce new family members to the wonderful person whom they'll never get to meet. My first thought was of sharing stories of Tris with future grandbabies: *Did you know that your grandpa Tris used to . . .?* Again, my eyes filled. It won't be enough. But it'll be all that we have.

Over the rest of the weekend, I had the chance to attend multiple workshops presented by similarly inspirational presenters. One made a particular impression. She had lost her partner seventeen years earlier in the 9/11 attacks; her fiancé was a first responder whose body had never been recovered. When this 9/11 widow described her grief, it was clear that she had been absolutely crushed, devastated. She'd been forever changed. At the same time, she described some of the ways she had coped with loss and rebuilt her life, which now involved marriage and mothering two children. Her workshops, "Making Butter" and "Exploring Sex, Safely," invited me to reflect on aspects of a future which I had not yet considered. Both presentations authentically addressed serious topics while also integrating humor and music.

This widow was resilient yet wholly vulnerable. Total strangers asked intimate questions about her experiences. She responded fully, without hesitation. I was overwhelmed with her generosity and love for a room of strangers who were full of need, full of doubts. She was a role model—a true inspiration. My feelings of admiration crystallized at the final camp banquet. At a nearby table, during the memorial ritual, this inspirational role model widow sobbed openly, shoulders heaving. Although she was undeniably strong and courageous, although she had moved on in her life and now led the way for me and for countless others, she also remained steadfast in her devotion to her lost love.

Other contradictory truths I encountered that weekend also remained with me. To feel the joy, we have to sit with the sadness. Sadness doesn't diminish joy. Rather, sadness sharpens joy. As the camp director said, "The darker the night, the brighter the stars." Another presenter suggested that our emotional experiences can be understood in terms of a mathematical function, represented as an oscillating sine wave. The greater our experience of sadness and despair, the greater access we have to joy and wonder. This metaphor matched with my constant sense of being on a roller coaster, riding the wave, continuously encountering unpredictable moments during which my heart drops, then lifts. Uncertainty is the only certainty.

Nothing is simple. Nothing is straightforward. I have all the feelings, all the time. Good news can't be shared with Tris, which creates sorrow. At the same time, he is spared terrible news, which creates relief. He should be here. He is not. The world is a dimmer place. Yet, there's still light.

CAMP WIDOW, PART THREE
The End

Camp Widow ended with a banquet dinner and dance—a Spring Fling. Perhaps intentionally, this event was not unlike a wedding. There was a cash bar. We selected entrees of chicken or beef. Round tables surrounded a dance floor and stage complete with a DJ and music equipment.

On each table, in addition to place settings and bread baskets, there were materials for the final memorial activity: black Sharpie markers and green plastic lily pads crowned by colorful lotus blossoms. As instructed, I wrote my name on the top of a lily pad and carefully wrote my beloved's name on the bottom. The camp director explained that our person is the foundation of the love and growth and beauty that is us, symbolized by the flower on top.

As soon as I finished writing my beloved's name, grief hit me hard. The sensation was painful and cerebral, like I had suddenly smacked my forehead into an invisible emotional wall. Looking at his name released something that had been tightly coiled up over the past three days, or perhaps even longer. During the different workshops over the course of the weekend, there had been moments during which my eyes teared and my throat ached in response to hearing others' stories—feeling for them and also for myself. My responses had been intense and brief. But throughout the hallways, restaurants, and other spaces, I'd also consistently witnessed less fleeting emotional intensity. Everywhere, it seemed, widows were weeping. Voices shook and were suddenly silenced as, mid-sentence, words were swallowed by sobs. I sympathized with these obvious moments of struggle. Before this moment, though, my grief had felt less raw, more remote.

I had assumed that this feeling of difference, of separation, was due to differences in our circumstances. Many of the people whom I met had suffered horrific losses, some of which were haunting, almost unimaginable. I had befriended a woman whose husband had died alone in a hotel room out of state while on a business trip. I befriended another woman whose stepdaughter of thirty-plus years sued her for a greater share of inheritance. Over the course of the weekend, I met people whose spouses died in sudden tragedy: by fire, by plane crash, by military combat, by terrorism. I met people whose spouses died by suicide. I met a person whose teen was imprisoned after being convicted of maternal homicide; in one tragic event, this person had lost both a spouse and a child.

My story was different from these stories, from other stories. Yet in a way, our stories were all the same. As the opening speaker said, we are a diverse community of unique individuals from different walks of life. Still, we're all joined by the shared experience of now sleeping in a bed in which our person is no longer there. We've all been propelled against our wills into a group that none of us had ever wanted to join, a stigmatized identity tainting each of us as incomplete. We've each been forced to confront unanswerable questions, including: *What am I supposed to do now?*

Helplessly, I cried, unable to speak. I reached for the hand of a kind older woman from Texas seated to my right. Her soft fingers were cool and comforting. To my left was a kind younger woman from Florida. She wrapped her arm around my shoulder, murmuring, "We've got you." I nodded, still voiceless. I knew. They did.

After what felt like an eternity, the wave had mostly passed. In the aftermath, along with a dull and lingering ache, I felt a deep gratitude to have immediate, accessible support from people who understood the pain: intense, intermittent, unavoidable, uncontrollable. The pain needed to be borne. It will continue to need to be borne. The only way forward is through.

Each person in the room, almost three hundred widows and widowers, walked up to the front. We merged from different lives, different circumstances, and different places to ultimately find ourselves in the same place. Once there, we formed a single line. Some of us were hugging, arms wrapped around one another. Some of us walked with heads bowed low, shoulders slumped. Some of us were tearful. Some of us were stoic. One by one, we each approached the person on the stage who held a microphone. One by one, we each said the name of our person aloud so everyone present could hear and bear witness and honor each person—each life now lost, each love that still remained.

I said his name. *Tristram.* My voice sounded unexpectedly foreign, a thin alto. Apparently, I'd been holding my breath.

Continuing on to the side of the room, I knelt to release our lotus flower, an emblem of our love, into one of the round, green ponds of shining water. The overhead lights shimmered in the smooth, reflective surface. The flowers swirled: red, yellow, pink, and blue. These symbols of our loved ones and our eternal devotion floated—individual flowers commingling, joining other individual flowers, budding into clusters until the ponds overflowed, blooming with colors and memories, brightness and love.

Birthday Letter

Dearest Tris,

Happy birthday, darling. Today you would've been fifty-eight. You've been gone for eight months and three days.

I go to the drugstore and find the aisle with cards. I start to read: "Each day we are together, I cherish you" and "You make my life complete." Immediately I start to cry, chest heaving. Sobs escape from my throat. Although I'm making a scene, I don't care. Someone walks by. I look down at the rack of cards as if I'm alone in the aisle, in the store, in the world.

Many of the cards are beautiful. Some are fancy, with script and lace. Other cards are cute. They feature small animals or beloved characters. *Hello, Mickey Mouse. Hello, Dora the Explorer.* I trace the outlines with my index finger. These adorable cards express love in simple terms. They're full of joy. But a few cards express sadness or irritable grumbling about growing older. One shows a man being chased by candles. Another asks if time can halt, if birthdays can stop. Unexpectedly, I'm furious. Didn't the authors of these cards consider the alternative, what it actually means to stop having birthdays, to stop aging?

So far, every birthday card has been written in the present tense. Is this the wrong tense? I search for cards that can still work, still apply. Finally, I select a card for you. It's small and beige with geometric shapes. The front shows a round green treetop on a rectangle brown trunk. I hear your voice, "Jenny always likes leaves." *Yes, always.* Two bright turquoise bluebirds face each other, seated on the ground. They appear to be enjoying the shade, enjoying one another. The front of the card says, "You're the bright spot in more days than I can count." The inside of the card is beige and green. It says, "So happy to celebrate all the wonderful things you are to me. Happy Birthday with Love." Once home, I'll carefully address the card to you.

I look at cards the children might sign for your birthday. I don't know if they'll want to. But if they do, they should have options. One smaller card features three cartoon fish standing on a podium, the type offered to Olympic medalists. The fish are white, blue, and lavender. Each wears a gold, silver, or bronze medal on a red ribbon necklace. Each has fins on hips: looking up, smiling, bubbles floating overhead. Inside, the card says, "Best fishes on your birthday!" This seems perfect. You ate fish but no meat—and you loved puns. And we are now a family of three.

The other card is large and pastel, mostly light pink, edged on the bottom with blue and yellow stripes. It features characters from Charlie Brown: a smiling Lucy embracing Snoopy, arms looped around his neck. Their eyes are closed. Although Lucy rarely smiles, she is beaming! The front reads, "Happy Birthday with Love." The inside says, "You are loved for who you are—someone unique and beautiful and totally herself. Hope you know that you deserve all the happiest things in life, today and always." I'm slow to realize that this pink card is meant for a girl or a woman. Still, it's perfect. Is anyone more deserving of the happiest things, today and always? We always loved watching the Charlie Brown holiday cartoons, trying to mimic the muffled adult voices and searching for the most pathetic, crooked, sad Charlie Brown type shrub at the Christmas tree lot.

I decide we need a candle we can light to honor you. I consider the available options and settle on Creamy Vanilla Coconut. The candle smells sweet, like a birthday, and also like fruit, which you loved. You didn't love scented candles, so I hesitate . . . but the candle's soft white hue feels sacred, and therefore correct. Next, I walk around, eager to find other small gifts to buy. I pick out two candy bars. Snickers were your favorite. Sometimes when you were alive, if I was at the drugstore, I'd buy you a Snickers for a surprise treat. Now that you're gone, the candy aisle evokes tears. No longer can I bring this to you, a small surprise—your eyes lighting up, gentle smile on your lips, your joy lifting my heart.

A dear friend left me a card for this occasion, for your birthday, knowing that we'd be tearful, missing you. It shows colorful flamingos, wings spread, moving in swirling pools of blue water. The front says, "We can't always choose the music life plays for us, but we can choose how we dance to it." The inside says, "so let the music play."

Tonight we'll have a celebratory dinner in your honor. We'll sign cards for you. We'll light a candle. We may even sing.

Happy birthday, dearest man.

Love,
Jenny

Mother's Day

In two days, it will be Mother's Day—my first as a single mom. You've been gone for just over nine months.

Before we were together, I never thought I'd actually be someone's *mother*. Motherhood felt too sacrificial, too limiting. And it felt like an overwhelming amount of work, of responsibility, with perilously high stakes. Recently and apparently randomly, our daughter, now sixteen, expressed new insight on this topic. "Mom!" she said. "Being a parent is a *LOT* of work. You're basically teaching a person how to *LIVE A LIFE*. That's a big job!" Our daughter is wise. She's like you, in so many ways.

When we were mere acquaintances—coworkers at the same institution—you seemed shy and serious. So it was fascinating when you brought your six-year-old son to picnics and parties. With Jonah, you were silly and fun. The two of you collected bugs for his science kit. You splashed one another in the pool. You wore matching costumes.

Before you and I decided to be a couple, we talked about parenting. It was our third date. Jonah was away. You cooked me a multiple course Italian dinner: soup, chicken, and cannoli for dessert. Before we ate, you gave me a tour of your home. Jonah's room was filled with books and toys. The bathtub literally overflowed with ducks, boats, and other floaties. As a dad, your generosity shone.

After dinner, in the living room, the light was low. You spoke haltingly. You said you wanted me to be your girlfriend. You also said that, because you were infertile and I deserved to be with someone who could give me babies, I should probably just go home.

All of this was highly unexpected. *Girlfriend? Infertile? Go home?*

My heart and brain shifted, aligned with new joyous possibility. You were a renowned child psychologist. Who would be a better partner and co-parent? *Jonah could be mine, too.* Plus, you were a secret goofball: you told knock-knock jokes and won at ping pong. Parenting felt not only possible. It felt fun.

I blurted out, "But I don't want to be pregnant. Ever."

You looked amazed. Slowly, I told you of my hidden wish to adopt a child who needed a home. I worried about balancing work and family, about being a good enough mom. But this was my secret dream. Eyes shining, you said, "I always wanted two kids. We could adopt!"

And we did. Because of you, I'm a mother.

For almost two decades, when you were by my side, I looked forward to Mother's Day with eager anticipation. Every year, you spent hours taking photos to document our family life. Each April, you spent hours carefully selecting and arranging photos, captioning each with dates and funny phrases. Every Mother's Day, either after a fancy brunch or before a fancy dinner, you'd present me with a gift: a photo album of the past year. Together, our family would review each photo, each page—reminiscing and laughing about our vacations and time spent with beloved relatives and friends.

Not everything in our family, as reflected in our photo albums, was always perfect. In some photos, some of us might look goofy, perhaps with double chins or deranged expressions. Occasionally, one of us would complain about unflattering light or unfortunate camera angles. You'd smile and shrug. You'd say, "I did my best."

And you did. We were the luckiest family.

This year, I look forward to Mother's Day with both sorrow and gratitude. In this saddest of seasons, a time newly without you, I have our two amazing children. I'm bereft—yet blessed.

DNA

When my husband died about ten months ago, people seemed to know that this was a tragedy. They knew that my heart was now shattered, my life now tilted. Losing a husband is seen as a major loss even though (most) husbands and wives aren't considered to be family based on shared genes, blood ties, or DNA. In our marriage, as in most marriages, the deep and enduring bond between us developed because we'd chosen one another.

One reason that losing a husband is seen as a major loss is this: traditionally, a woman is expected to marry a man. Marriage to a man legitimizes womanhood. Traditionally, this man is taller, stronger, richer and, of course, older. A certain type of age difference is expected. I'm now newly aware of how this expectation for older men to pair with younger women puts women at risk for widowhood.

A legitimate woman is not only married; she also conceives and bears children. So, when I talk about or show photos of my stepson or adopted daughter, others often ask, "But do you have any kids of your own?" When I respond, "They are my own," their smiles fade. This isn't, biologically speaking, a legitimate answer. In our culture, *real* motherhood is predicated on sharing a genetic bond with children who share your DNA, your flesh and blood.

Since my husband died, multiple people have warned that my connection with my stepson Jonah is now tenuous, at risk. They don't understand. One support group counselor starkly informed me that, now that his father is gone, my stepson and I would no longer be close. Lasting family bonds and true intimacy stem from blood ties, she lectured. She seemed unaware of how ironic this statement must sound to a grieving widow.

She was wrong. Jonah is in my heart, forever. He was my first child, my only boy—and now he's a man. He was six when we met, eight when we became family. When his dad and I told him we wanted to marry, initially, Jonah expressed concerns: "But you don't have a tuxedo! And you don't have a dress." We assured him these matters were easily resolved. He nodded slowly. Then he took my hand and showed me all of his secret hiding places.

Since then, Jonah and I have spent countless hours together. Before he left for college, we shared a home for ten years. We've sat together in airports, auditoriums, bistros, and buses. We've shared space in cars, churches, classrooms, and clinics. We've enjoyed picnics, parties, restaurants, and recitals. We've discussed food and family, politics and philosophy, rock music and romance. I've planned his birthdays, chaperoned school trips, cheered his baseball team, folded his socks, and checked his homework. He taught me to shoot baskets, to tie a tie, and to use my first cell phone. When I was bedridden after an accident, ten-year-old Jonah came to my room and played the clarinet for me. *My very own concert, every night!*

Jonah visited his mom for six weeks each summer, for school breaks, and for alternating holidays. Each time, the separation was hard. Each time, I waited as patiently as I could for him to come home.

One summer, a little girl in our neighborhood asked me where Jonah was. She hadn't seen him lately. I told her Jonah was visiting his mom. "His *mom?!* Then who are you?" She stared at me with dis-appointment and suspicion—an imposter, revealed. So, I told her the real story. Once upon a time, we didn't have very much money. We were hungry. Our pantry was almost bare and there wasn't enough food for everyone. So, I led Jonah away into the forest so he would get lost and never return. Then I ate all of our bread and cheese myself.

She laughed. I was relieved that she got the joke.

Soon after his dad died, Jonah turned twenty-seven years old. It felt like a closing of a loop, a circle of time. When I was twenty-seven, I became his stepmother and took on much new responsibility. As it turned out, at that same age, Jonah also took on much new responsibility, and for another family transition: the loss of his father. It's hard to imagine the aftermath of Tris's death without Jonah's support and love. As the step-/parent, I wanted him to be able to lean on me. At times, I think he did. But there were many, many times when, instead, I leaned on him. Together we cleaned out the kitchen and the basement. In the office, Jonah "hacked" his dad's computer to find out his passwords for accounts. He replaced all of the electrical outlets that weren't up to code. He labeled each of the different boxes of light bulbs, so I'd know where and how to replace them. He taught me basic kitchen skills and bought me supplies: a rice cooker, a meat thermometer, a cookbook. When Maddy and I called, slightly hysterical about a mouse in the kitchen, he calmly outlined options for traps.

Early in the summer, Jonah helped me clear the disorderly, untidy yard. Together we pulled at the vines that crawled up, over, and across the house—having snaked behind screens, under the siding, choking the foundation. We uprooted the bed of dirt, sod, and weeds that had completely overtaken the back steps. Together we cleared away the debris, the remnants of past seasons, past storms.

Sometimes, when Jonah comes home, he sits in his father's chair while he sips coffee and reads the news. Seeing him there takes my breath away. He embodies his father at the same time that he is his own person, separate and independent. He is deep and wise. He is caring and kind. When I make mistakes, he is calm and patient. He laughs at me gently, completely without malice, for the same reasons his father did: I can be concrete, careless, inflexible, irritating. He doesn't seem to mind. He's a role model for my daughter, his sister, as well as for me, his stepmother. As our roles shift, our family bonds remain sturdy, solid, and strong.

Once upon a time, I was overly dismissive of the blood ties of family, the genetic bonds of DNA. There are other paths to kinship. People can be bonded emotionally without genetic ties—like Jonah and Maddy and me. People also can be bonded genetically without emotional intimacy—like my father and his estranged children. Yet now that Tris has died, I newly appreciate both kinds of bonds. Both kinds of bonds can connect families to each other. Both kinds of bonds can connect us to those who are no longer with us.

Both of my children resemble their father. Both share his wisdom, his kindness, his sturdiness. Tris shaped their minds and hearts. And they'll carry on his legacy. But only Jonah bears Tris's physical resemblance: the shape of the chin, the facial expression, the sweet smile. In these specific ways, as the psychic medium had forecasted, Jonah "wears" his father. Especially now that Tris is gone, I find myself unexpectedly grateful and humbled by the power of DNA, for those moments when I can still catch a glimpse of my beloved husband.

Tend and Befriend

The week after his death, I hung photos of Tris all around the house. Some were family portraits. Other photos featured him and me, the happy couple. There were also pairings of Tris with each child at different ages. These pictures helped remind us of him. *He's still here, with us, even if not physically.*

About six months later, these photos seemed somehow fraudulent. They seemed to belong to a different world, a different reality. In fact, he is no longer here. In this new world, he is gone. He is no longer here, in our home, where I now feel alone, lost, and, irrationally, homeless.

During the week of what would have been our nineteenth wedding anniversary, an overnight visitor arrived. In passing, she mentioned that she's never been away from her spouse for more than a week. I realized then that my current separation from Tris had also been our longest. It's growing. And it's permanent. There will be no sweet reunion: no kiss hello—head tilted up, embracing his shoulders.

About ten months after Tris's death, leaving the children's rooms untouched, I began to remove the photos from the walls, storing them carefully out of sight. I removed the wedding photos from their frames. Then I carefully stored these, along with anniversary cards and love letters, in a beautiful purple box for safekeeping. Photos can be kept safe, even if people can't.

In the field of psychology, special words describe different aspects of grief and our adaptation to it. Grief involves a ruptured *attachment bond*. Tris and I were once tethered together but the link is now tattered, frayed, flying loose. I feel a deep yearning to be close to him, for *proximity*. I feel *separation anxiety*, a form of stress that feels unresolvable after someone dies. Because I want what I can't have, there is always pain. The pain connects me to my love. And when the pain is less sharp, I feel less connected. Does this mean there is nowhere to go? Does this mean there's no way to feel better? Does feeling better always mean also feeling worse?

In grief, I'm learning to stay connected to my late husband, even though he's gone. The connection is internal and intangible. It's emotional, not physical. It's spiritual, sacred, not of this world. To let go of our physical, worldly connections doesn't mean we don't care, as one counselor patiently explained. Rather, letting go means deciding to live in peace. And in this different world with an intangible connection to Tris, I need new attachments, new affectionate bonds with others who can see me, hear me, and hug me.

Tend and befriend is a stress response that involves developing warm relationships with others. It includes meeting new people. It also includes relating to others in caring, meaningful ways. Tend and befriend has never before been my way. I've always been socially reticent, shy. *Don't bother people. They are busy. They are important. Don't waste their time. Don't waste time.* That voice in my head first called out in early childhood with a non-subtle subtext: *They are important; you are not.*

In a wonderful marriage, now over—but, still, with my children, with friends, with many colleagues and students—I've been lucky enough to feel at least somewhat important, at least in my own way. But importance usually felt tied to getting things done. Producing. Giving. Completing. Sending. Checking the task off the list. Making a new list. Make a list of the lists. We're all busy. Time spent talking to people is time away from productivity, accomplishment, achievement.

Now, in grief, I'm opening up, reaching out. An invisible hand guides me to new behaviors, places, and relationships. No longer am I just doing. I'm being and being with others in new ways.

I attend a yoga class. The teacher's words touch my heart. She calls for us to relax and breathe, to notice when we feel pain, to acknowledge what is happening so that we can figure out what to do next. I pause after class, telling her that her words restore my spirit during a difficult time. I don't elaborate with details. The details don't matter. She hugs me. We're now connected in a new way.

I attend a writing grief group. The teacher generously invites me to send her more writings even after the class has ended. I pick one that I think she'll like. It turns out, for entirely different reasons, it was the perfect choice. I'm overwhelmed to be able to give back, in a small way, to this compassionate and loving person who has helped me so much. We're now connected in a new way.

I have a new friend. We have coffee, lunch. We grumble about trying to teach our teens to drive. This friend later, unexpectedly, tells me about having a hard day, about feeling down and blue. I'm struck by how much I care. "Can I come over?" I ask. I go. We sit together. We're now connected in a new way.

I have an old friend. She's smart and fun, although we've never been emotionally close. She tells me about a difficult situation at work. I offer support. Later, I send her an essay in which I described facing something similar long ago. She responds with encouragement. For the first time ever, she expresses love. We're now connected in a new way.

I reach out. I try to be with others, to tend and befriend. Through communion, I try to love. I try to heal.

REFLECTING ON LOVE

- What are some of the different ways that you honor your loved one on holidays and other special or milestone days?

- How is your experience of grief affected by your beliefs about the spiritual world? What are your beliefs about the afterlife? In what ways do you find yourself reaching out to your loved one? How do you stay connected?

- Given that grief often involves conflicting emotions (e.g., sadness coupled with relief that a loved one isn't suffering), how do experiences of positive emotions affect your experiences of negative emotions? And how do negative emotions affect positive ones? When do these feelings coexist rather than cancel one another out? Under what circumstances do you find yourself most strongly pulled between positive and negative emotions?

- Have you participated in grief groups or other loss-based communities? If so, how have these communities made you feel? When does being with other bereaved people help you feel less alone? And when does being with other bereaved people *not* ease your sense of loneliness?

- Do you see traces of your loved one in people who are still in the world? Which people show these traces—and how? How do you personally embody your loved one's behaviors, attitudes, values, and other qualities?

- How has loss affected your relationships with other people? In what ways are other people helping you feel less alone or less overwhelmed? In what ways is spending time with other people newly challenging?

PART III
Halting Steps Forward

At first, the pain that came with loss felt entirely unbearable. Knowing that my late husband had always wanted my happiness helped me to expand in love. Eventually, I began to embrace life as a single woman, although moving forward in these ways felt halting, at best.

My earliest attempts to relate to new romantic partners sparked shame and sadness, happiness and hope. Dating filled me with nostalgia for the past while also inspiring new possibilities. Some men were judgmental or predatory. Others were generous and compassionate. Regardless, all of these interactions taught me to honor what lingered: my identify, my life, my future.

Connections with potential new partners carried me through milestone moments in consistently awkward, mostly tenuous, sometimes comical ways. The essays here highlight an array of confusing dating experiences—many involving first steps: the first date, the first second date, the first kiss. These interactions, for better and for worse, helped me accept and cope with my new reality.

Release

My husband died. A sudden heart attack ended his life, turning my world upside down. Afterward my muscles, including my own heart, became twisted and tense, coiled and cold.

The sadness wasn't without sweetness. I'm beyond grateful to have had a great love. Tris had made my dreams come true. Because of him, I became a mother. Because of him, I felt accepted, adored, and admired. He loved me more than anyone else ever had. He was truly an exceptional man: kind, funny, brilliant. He laughed when I was annoying. He teased me for being impatient. He saw all of me, my heart and my shadow, but never flinched. He believed that he was the lucky one in our relationship. But I knew better.

Losing a great love is indescribably sad. For the first time, I truly grasped the word "tragedy." Beyond the sadness, grief felt like tension mixed with despair. Grief felt like perpetual, muscular, embodied frustration. *Tris isn't here.* I can't ask him about lawn care or about the strange medicines in the lower drawer. I can't ask him about our teen daughter's new boyfriend. I can't tell him about my latest publication or about our grown son's search for a new job. I can't tell him about the end of the audiobook that we'd been listening to: Ben Rhodes's memoir, *The World as It Is.*

I can't see him. I can't smell him. I can't touch him, feel him. I stay up until all hours to avoid our cold, empty bed.

It's all unbearable but it must be borne. So, I pretended. *Everything's fine! He's in my heart and in my children, so he's not really gone.* A few weeks in, when I actually caught myself waiting to hear his key in the lock, I forced myself to remove the ring from my left hand. My bare finger was slightly dented, misshapen after almost nineteen years of embrace. I confessed to Jonah, my oldest child, an adult man who is now fatherless. He said, "You don't have to do this." I cried and did it anyway.

At work, I also pretended. People gazed at me oddly from their office chairs. Some asked directly, "Why are you *here*?" But I craved work. Because Tris had never walked these hallways, here, I didn't feel his absence so acutely. At times, the pretense was so convincing that people sometimes complained to me. They were stressed about deadlines and garage doors. Their pets misbehaved. I sympathized but privately marveled at how intact their lives seemed to be.

At times, I was even so convincing that I fooled myself. *Everything's fine!* I had to remind myself why my closest friends brought us food and flowers, why they were being so nice.

At other times, I couldn't pretend. At yoga, teachers routinely instructed, "Connect with your inner self." When I did, tears leaked from my eyes. My breath shifted and quickened. I gulped air, trying to remain quiet as a flood of painful feelings washed over me. I kept my eyes closed. I stretched and bent. The tears leaked when a soft song played. The tears leaked during final resting pose. I tried to breathe. "Release the tension," the teacher would say. But I could not.

When the year ended, I realized that there would be a new year without Tris in the world. This seemed impossible. How could this be? My heart was frozen, an internal tundra. It was winter in the world and in my body. There was no warmth. There was no relaxation. No wine, chocolate, pleasure, sleep. There was no release. The sun still rose and set. The clock hands continued to tick forward. My jaw clenched. The circles deepened under my eyes. I couldn't stop time.

⟡

Eventually, after more time passed, I decided to try to embrace being single. This was my new identity. And single people meet other single people. They do this through dating. I'll meet my tribe: "Hello! Here I am!" I'll present myself as whole and intact. In so doing, somehow, someday, I'll become whole and intact. *In no time*, I thought, *I'll be complaining about deadlines and my garage door.*

I did an internet search to learn about online dating options. I chose a site recommended for widows, but the site required a photo. *Ugh.* I took a selfie in the hallway, trying to imitate a happy person with a bright smile. But the only brightness was the shine on my nose and forehead. There was sort of a smile there. *Good enough.* I uploaded the photo and started to write a self-description but didn't know what to say. *Some of my favorite things: the color green, the scent of lavender, the taste of strawberries.* Truly, I had no idea what I was doing.

Immediately, my attention was fractured by messages. I felt circled, as if by wolves. I replied to each, "I'm not ready, not in the same place, you seem great, but we aren't a match." Most argued. They told me I needed a positive person. Desperate, I played my widow card. I revealed that I was new to the site; my husband had died. But some wolves persisted, newly inspired. They told me that they were divorced, and they don't see their kids every day and those are all "the same" as losing a husband. Loss is loss. They said or implied that I was being difficult, that I didn't even want to try. Which was true, of course.

From within my heart, Tris shook his head. "Beautiful Jenny," he whispered. "No. No. None of these will do." I felt him speak to me—just as I felt the knot in my shoulder, the tension in my jaw, the clenching in my gut.

A possible non-wolf asked to meet for drinks. I confessed to

Maddy, my youngest child, an adolescent who is now fatherless. I asked her permission to get this first "date" over with. She said, "You don't have to do this." I cried and did it anyway. Then I met the person. He seemed . . . okay. He was full of compliments. He said he liked my smile. He expressed reassurance, "You're doing great." I felt flattered. This was a surprising feeling. But I didn't really like him. He talked for almost an hour about how people fail to act how he wants them to act. He wanted people to be different. He wanted the world to be different. I got it. I did. In him, this unhappiness, this dissatisfaction looked and felt like anger. In me, it looked and felt like tension. I played my widow card. At least initially, he seemed to accept it. Flooded with shame, I told a close friend that I went on a first "date." She looked at me with affection, eyes shining. She told me that she loves me. I was grateful as I cried, rolling my neck around my tight shoulders.

જ

Some time passed before I met anyone who seemed likeable. His first message was short: "Lavender. . . yes." This was different. He had read my profile to learn about me. I looked at his profile. There was a lot there. "PBJ-Yum!" I replied. He responded instantly, "So I'm thinking we'll serve PB-Strawberry jelly sandwiches on green plates, set on tables adorned with bouquets of lavender, at our wedding. Is that agreeable to you? Oh, I'm Charles. Will you marry me?"

He was funny and outrageous. He showed that he'd read my list of favorite things. I praised him, "Wow! A dream wedding. You're GOOD." Our chatting continued. He concluded with, "I think your profile is delightful and sweet. Would you be interested in talking again?" The next day he sent a new message: "Are you still in love with me? Were you impressed at how smoothly I introduced love into the equation without you ever having professed it for me? I learned it in the book *The Art of Manipulation for People Who Are Overtly Honest.*"

Unexpectedly, I was charmed: "It's pretty fantastic how you consistently blend authenticity with the absurd." Then he gave me his number and invited me to text or call him. Anytime. I was surprised by the feeling between us. Was this . . . *chemistry?* How was that possible?

Charles seemed to read me, to know how skittish I was, to recognize how I was just trying out being single. Again, he invited me to reach out, via phone or text, whenever I wanted. We spoke on the phone. His voice was deep. He talked a lot—and quickly, at least at first. He wanted me to know about him. He told me that he lives a couple of hours away and asked if that's okay. I secretly cheered. Distance felt safe. He was witty, sharp. I took note. He asked about Tris. I carelessly revealed how much I loved my husband and the many positive ways Tris changed my life. This conversation didn't feel awkward. In fact, Charles seemed to like hearing this.

Charles seemed reassuring and non-demanding: "Do you want to talk about this? Are you tired? Should I let you go?" We talked for two hours. The time flew by. Amazed, I found myself giddy. He seemed giddy, too. After we hung up, I fell into a restless sleep. The next night we talked again. After a first late night, we were both exhausted. I had set a time limit to talk for less than forty minutes but then changed my mind. I didn't want to hang up, so didn't.

The next night Charles texted me while I was browsing in a bookstore with my daughter. He told me he was in town and heading to his hotel. He asked if he could text me after he got settled. My face flushed bright and hot. I felt flooded with conflicting emotions and thoughts: suspicion and fear mixed with unexpected feelings of longing. *What's going on?* Why is he here? Does he want money? To convert me to a religion—a cult? To trick me in some way? I was terrified to meet him. I yearned to meet him. I felt like I missed him. But did I? I missed Tris. I missed Tris so much. These were conflated feelings, right? Classic displacement.

My daughter had been born halfway around the world. Before I met her, before our adoption was finalized, I had missed her. I had missed her with a ferocity that seemed inexplicable and irrational. But it was real. What is real? Now, with Tris dead, I missed him fiercely. And now I felt like I missed Charles. But did I? Or did I miss the person who I could reach out to, the one who could respond?

Back at home, my feelings led me to my own bookshelf. Tris had given me a book just a couple of months before he died. There's a quote in it that I felt I needed to find. The book, *Here if You Need Me*, is by a widow who writes about loss and renewal. For possibly mystical reasons, Tris bought it for me last summer. He even had it signed by the author, Kate Braestrup. I had read it on Christmas Day—this one last gift, from Tris, to me. I found the quote:

"Your heart is not a stone. True love demands that, like a bride with her bouquet, you toss your fragile glass heart into the waiting crowd of living hands and trust that they will catch it."

Fragile glass heart? Yes. I felt like I needed some space to think.

Several days passed. Later in the week, Charles and I texted one another. I tried to guess his astrological sign but was supremely incompetent. Repeatedly, I tried and failed to spell the word "Sagittarius." We laughed and laughed; my belly ached. And then there was a shift, a more serious feel. He said he was "sweet on me." He said he understood that Tris would always be in my heart. He said he could be patient. Things could move slowly.

Again, I said I needed a few more days of space. I didn't reach out to him, although at times, I wanted to. I wanted to say: *I miss you and also I miss Tris. And these seem related.* I also wanted to send him the quote, the one about the glass heart. But I didn't.

The next time we talked, it felt more serious. I asked for his last name. I invited him to meet me for a first date in six weeks. *Surely, I'd feel ready by then?* I told him that Tris wanted me to learn to like surprises, so he could decide what would be fun and surprise me. I asked him to tell me when the plans were made. He did. A plan was set for us to meet.

When I woke up the next morning, the bedroom looked different. Why? I didn't know. But unexpectedly, the room felt cluttered. I looked around and saw my surroundings in a new light. Tris had died almost immediately after returning home from a trip. His open suitcase still sat atop the dresser. Clothes had been piled on top of and next to the suitcase. His huge tower of clothes in need of dry cleaning had been heaped on a chair.

I began to clear the clothes. I began to cry hot tears. My face flushed.

I folded each pair of pants, staining them with tears, stroking them with love. I picked a few to keep for the laundry. I put the shorts and pants on my own legs, feeling them. The rest I folded into bags for charity, to donate someday—when it feels right. I cried and cried. I made space for the sadness, and also, for the newness.

There was, at last, the start of a shift: a hint of release.

⚬

I ended up meeting Charles for lunch. It didn't go well. In person, we struggled to connect. He felt stiff and remote. Overall, he seemed disappointed. To be honest, I felt disappointed as well. Still, I was grateful to him. Our phone conversations began to offer me a new outlook. Our conversations gave me practice. Our conversations gave me the start of a new feeling: hope.

How to Date a Widow

Please, ask me about my late husband. You won't make me sad or ruin the mood. He is here, with us, whether or not you ask. Remember, he's not my "ex." We never divorced. Words matter. Use his name. If he comes up, don't quickly change the subject. Show that you feel for me as a fellow human—one with a heart, one who has endured a terrible, sudden loss.

Try to catch yourself before you make assumptions about what I need and how fragile or incapable I am. I may need help. If so, I may ask. But before you decide on your own that I need protection, advice, or someone to clean out the gutters, don't forget to notice: I'm still standing upright even though the ground completely dropped out from under my feet. Apparently, I can fly!

My love for my late husband is a gift to us both. There's absolutely nothing for you to fear. Don't be intimidated or threatened. If you're into me, you're in luck! Because of the great love I've tasted, great love is inside me now. I know how to keep interested and invested, how to accept and give freely, how to love joyfully and without condition. I know how to argue and stay on the same team. I know how to focus on what matters. What matters now is how you treat me, care for me, and respect me. This includes your ability to receive my generosity. I'm looking for mutuality, reciprocity—a partner, not a child—and definitely *not* a father. Your height and size and eye color are irrelevant. Your education and job title don't matter. I don't care how much money you do or don't have. I care about your depths, your heart, your very soul.

My heart has room to carry my old loves and to grow to encompass new love. There are many important people in the world and in each of our lives. I don't believe we each get just one soulmate. We meet many different people for different reasons and at different points in time. All of them matter. There's no competition among meaningful relationships. I've enjoyed wonderful caring friends, not just one best one, and I've been closer to some than others at different stages in my life. I've enjoyed multiple caring lovers; my wonderful relationship with my late husband doesn't erase the passion, still accessible, for my first high school love. If I find new love and passion, new buds in my heart will flower, bloom, and multiply.

Know that I'm now a single mom and that my children continue to be my world. They must be first, always. Know that I never wanted to parent alone and that it's terrifying. Bonus challenge: now alone, I parent grieving children while vulnerable with grief myself. When I attend a recital or get good news about her report card or his new job, I'm sad because my children no longer have all of the support and love they once had. I want to make up for this somehow but can't. Everything I do for them is less than what my late husband and I would have done together. I miss him selfishly and also for the sake of my children.

Know that when you talk about someone who has died, I automatically think of my late husband. Know that when you say it was hard to get over the loss of your mother, coworker, or friend, I'm full of sympathy. Also, at the same time, part of me plunges into my own private sadness.

Even in great tragedy, there is joy. My relationship with my late husband wasn't perfect. Your past relationships weren't perfect. You and I have both experienced joy, even if perhaps not enough. There were reasons for your past relationship: why you were first attracted, why you stayed together for as long as you did, why you moved out, why you filed for divorce. Maybe you were mistreated. Me, too, in some of my early relationships. We're all flawed people who do the best we can. Sometimes that isn't good enough. I've made mistakes, and I'll make more mistakes. But I won't intentionally mistreat you. We all have regrets. Living in regret is no way to be open to possibility. *Come, join me.* Openness is both terrifying and exhilarating.

Know that when you ask about my plans or what I'm looking for, there's no clear answer. There's no way to know. I'm not coy. I'm not withholding information. I'm an open book. Ask me, read me, see me. I'm looking to build a new life, rising from the ashes. I want to experience and share joy along with the inevitable hardships of life. I want to love. I want to matter.

My late husband wanted the best for me—always. I want to honor him and the time I have left in this world, however long that may be. I want to feel his joy when he sees me with someone who is generous and considerate, someone who thinks I'm funny and fierce, someone who feels lucky that we found each other.

Mr. Nice Guy

Before I'd even finished writing my profile description, as I signed up on an online dating website, a man contacted me to express interest. He was the first of many Nice Guys: good guys, guys who felt they'd been wronged. These guys put themselves out there looking for appreciation, for care, for connection. I could see what they wanted but felt unable to respond as they wished.

The very first Mr. Nice Guy told me that he saw from my (incomplete) profile that I didn't want to be involved with a smoker. In a highly transparent move, he admitted that he's a smoker. But he seemed to feel that his case was exceptional. The only reason he smokes, he said, is that he caught his now ex-wife cheating on him, which had been very stressful. He also said that he was trying to quit. I tried to respond with compassion and authenticity. I wished him well, expressing appreciation for his honesty and my belief that we weren't compatible. He indicated that I should get in touch if I changed my mind.

As I chatted with the hopeful smoker and struggled to find the words to complete my profile, Goodguy117 contacted me. Navigating simultaneous chat conversations with strange men felt overwhelming. Fortunately, Goodguy117 was direct and to the point. He asked what I was looking for. Taken aback, I answered truthfully, "I'm honestly not sure. I haven't dated in over twenty years."

"You haven't had a date in twenty years? Do you need training?

Lol. I'm not going to be your test dummy. I'm here for a relationship and connection. That means kissing and more. LOL. You ready for all that with a guy?"

Taken even more aback, I replied, "I'm sorry—I am not." This was my last message to him. Later, he replied with apparent anger, "Well, we could be friends but sounds like you don't even want that." He was correct, of course. A week or so later, out of the blue, he wrote again, "Are you still here looking around? Are you ready yet?"

Once complete, my profile included the fact that I'm the adoptive mom of an amazing high school student. A different Nice Guy reached out to ask if my teen was a girl or a boy. He suggested that the three of us could go bowling. I replied that I wouldn't be comfortable bringing my teen to meet a man I didn't yet know. He then suggested we have dinner together on Thursday or Friday. I apologized, being unavailable those nights, and offered to meet for coffee next Tuesday. His response: "Thursday or Friday."

I said that it seemed difficult for us to work out a common time. He suggested that he could bring me lunch at my place of work on either Thursday or Friday. I told him that I didn't think we were very compatible, because I wasn't looking for someone to interact with my child or my coworkers. Also, it seemed like he had a hard time taking "no" for an answer. He responded, "I'm sorry you feel that way. I was just trying to show you that I am family oriented." And that was that.

Another Nice Guy messaged me to ask about my relationship deal breakers. "Smoking," I stated happily, confidently. Here was a question that I knew how to answer! He agreed that smoking was a deal breaker for him, as well. Then he pressed on. "What else?" Good question. After some thought, I replied, "Well, racism, especially because my daughter is an immigrant." His response: "Have you ever been with a Black man?"

Shocked, I asked, "Do you mean dating?"

"Sex," he replied.

Even more shocked, I was overly revealing: "I've never been romantically or sexually involved with anyone who isn't white, and I'm not sure that's anything to be proud of." He challenged me. He said my response was untruthful, because he already knew that my daughter isn't white. Fully angered, I clarified that my daughter had been adopted from another country. His reply, now conciliatory, fully revealed what a poor fit he and I would be: "I knew that you were a good girl. Not a pig."

A different Nice Guy messaged me, asking what I'd like to do for a first date. He said he was open to suggestions but offered one of his own: "Maybe I could just hold you and we could see what happens next." Honestly, I didn't know what to say to this!

On a phone call, still another Nice Guy asked about my occupation. After I said that I taught at a local college, he paused and sighed. He told me that he'd previously been involved with a professor, and it hadn't gone well. Still, he was confident things would be "different" with me. I asked how he knew, silently reflecting on the many hours of grading and class preparation that affected time available to spend with my family. He hesitated and said that he wasn't comfortable elaborating, so we moved on. A few minutes later, out of the blue, he told me that the professor he'd dated wanted him to provide her with a specific type of sexual pleasure *every single time.* What she wanted—her demand for pleasure—was unacceptable to him. He sought to reassure me, though, repeating his expectation that this wouldn't be a problem for us.

Apparently, I was a human inkblot, a walking Rorschach test. Nice Guys make so many presumptions, projections.

Some men seemed to feel that one way to be a Nice Guy is to offer advice about how to live. Often, I received weather-related guidance: "Be sure to wear gloves and a coat today" or "Make sure you warm up your car before you drive it in the cold." Another theme involved dating itself: "Maybe you want to get off this website, because you don't need all of the male attention." This tendency to offer advice often worked in my favor. When I wanted to exit a conversation, I'd truthfully say how much I loved my late husband and how much I miss him. In most cases, the men would respond, concerned, that it might be too soon for me to be dating. When they'd say it sounded like I wasn't ready, I could thank them for being understanding. I felt authentic gratitude when I didn't hear back again. My hope is that they moved on to other women, possibly ones who might be more receptive.

But not everyone responded to my hesitation by offering me space. Some Nice Guys don't give up. Some decided that I need someone, and they are available. But their persistence isn't only on them. I didn't always handle these situations well. Especially early on, and especially after meeting in person, I had trouble saying directly, "I'm not interested." In some cases, I felt badly about letting them down. In other cases, I felt concerned about provoking anger; being direct didn't feel safe. Despite my resolve to be ethical and authentic, I've definitely been indirect. I've definitely made mistakes.

༄

Before we met in person, one man who contacted me seemed highly considerate. He told me his full name, first and last. He suggested I look him up on LinkedIn, verifying his identity and his career as a scientist. This seemed laudable. I agreed to meet him for a drink. I arrived on time to find him already waiting at the entrance. He approached as if to pounce. When he made a move to hug me, I offered my hand. When he used my first and last name, I was stunned. *How did he know?* After I asked, he disclosed that when you look up a person on LinkedIn, that person can look you up in return. Oh. *Hmmm.* So, had his considerate move actually been a trick?

Our meeting was fine, mostly. He talked a great deal. I listened, which he liked, and I found manageable. Although I was listening, half of my attention was focused on how surreal my life had become, the fact that I was on a date. My brain was repeatedly, stupidly, stuck in a groove: *I can't believe this is happening. I don't want this to be happening. Why is this even happening?* My date aimed for flattery. He said I was attractive and a good conversationalist. This seemed untrue, although I appreciated the encouragement. Still, he was too intense, too eager. At one point, he asked whether I enjoyed sex— "once the time was right and with the right person." Shocked, I didn't know what to say. He asked to take me to dinner in a few days on what would be his birthday. I demurred, then left. Later that night, he texted me: "Did you get home ok? I really had a great time."

I thanked him, complimenting his kindness. Idiotically, I suggested that we talk soon. "I am glad you had fun," he replied. "Let me know your schedule so we can go to dinner. Hugs Goodnight." I didn't respond. The next day, he followed with a cryptic message: "The trauma but my daughter went to school today. Hope you had a smooth morning." I told him that I was glad she made it to school, that I had a very restless night and that I needed time. He might want to ask someone else to dinner for his birthday. His response sounded hopeful: "I understand but am very sad. I hope you don't date anyone else until we can see where this goes."

I apologized and said I was overwhelmed. I said that maybe we could get coffee in a few weeks and that I had zero plans for other dates. "Ok. Whenever you are ready. I was so happy last night? Let me know how I can help you. Always happy to chat by phone too." I didn't answer. Still, he later added: "You are special." I thanked him, complimenting his kindness and acknowledging that this wasn't going as he had hoped. In hindsight, this response was a mistake. Silence would've been kinder, less misleading, because he maintained hope: "I didn't have expectations. I am still hopeful."

Then: "I hope you are having a good day." Two days passed. "How was your week? My daughter has another infection." One day after this last text, I told him that I was sorry to hear about his daughter. I added that I wasn't going to be available for the foreseeable future. I told him that I hoped he'd find someone amazing, thanked him for his understanding, and wished him all the best. He wrote back the next day:

"I can't imagine what you are going through. You are an amazing lady, and you took my breath away when we met. But you are clearly not ready to date. I so wish you were. If you need a friend, I can be that. You have my number."

From here on out, despite the barrage of messages, I stopped responding. But the next day he sent a very long, very detailed text about how his daughter's boyfriend broke up with her. It ended succinctly: "People suck." Yes, yes, I got the hint and I deserved it.

Eight days later he wrote again. "I hope you are staying warm." Seven days passed. "How are you doing?" Then two more. "Making an offer on a house." And another four. "Do you know the name of a good education advocate or lawyer?"

After three more days, after yet another message, I finally responded: "I'm sorry. I didn't mean to mislead you about where I am. I need space. Please let me reach out to you if I'm so inclined. Please don't reach out to me. I appreciate your understanding." He responded almost immediately. "Ok." I felt relieved to have been clear and unequivocal. Progress! But he continued to reach out sporadically, asking how I was, asking if he'd seen me in a local coffee shop. His final message arrived nearly six months after our face-to-face meeting. "I doubt that you care, but . . ." He was correct. That was as far as I read.

§

I made fewer mistakes with my first dinner date, a different man who was also highly persistent. In person, he was extremely short, with icy blue eyes. His interest in me was probably because he was slightly taller. Despite his stature, or perhaps as compensation for it, this man was intimidating and highly dominant. We met in the foyer of the restaurant. He reached for a hug. Although I offered my hand, he ignored this. Instead, he wrapped his arms around my torso, squeezing tightly.

During dinner, he spoke at length and asked no questions. Bored and uncomfortable, I itched to leave. When he was a teen, he said, he worked as a butcher. He then owned a meat market and went on to become a banker. After retiring, he did construction jobs on the side. He also went to college at some point, studying finance. It was all a bit fuzzy. He'd married and fathered a son who lived at home after earning a "useless" college degree. The pieces of this man's life story didn't fit together—but I didn't care enough to ask for clarification.

He ordered dark chocolate cake for dessert and repeatedly directed me to try some. He was persistent even after I told him that I don't eat dessert. Reluctantly, I dropped my fork onto a few semisweet, dirt-colored crumbs. The power struggle persisted. I asked to split the bill. He insisted on paying. I tried to argue the point but remain gracious. When the bill arrived, he pretended to scrutinize it with alarm. As his attempt at humor withered, my irritation grew.

He asked if he could call me again sometime. I felt intimidated and told him that I worked until at least 9:00 p.m. each night, hoping that he'd find such dedication to work unattractive. But I heard from him the next day: "Good morning. Thank you very much for meeting me last night. Looking forward to seeing you again. I will call you after 9." I didn't pick up the phone.

And the following day. "Good morning. Happy Sunday." I wrote back fifteen hours later, saying it'd been a tough day and that the coming week marked a major milestone of my late husband's passing. He responded: "I feel for you. Hang in there and try to remember all the good memories of him. I will be here for you. Hope to see and talk to you soon." He signed this message with his first name, written in CAPS. He did likewise the next day: "How was your day? I was thinking about you. Hope you are feeling better." And three days later:

"Good morning. How are you? I know you are still grieving, and I absolutely respect that. When is better to talk, tonight or tomorrow? Enjoy your day!"

The day after that: "What is your favorite place for tea?" I responded by telling him that I was sorry, that I didn't mean to mislead him, that I wasn't doing well. I needed space. Please let me reach out; please don't reach out to me. I closed by saying that I appreciated his understanding. He replied, thanking me and saying he was here if I needed a friend.

But he continued to send messages. At first, he simply asked how I was. When that didn't work, he told me he was "closing my file"—that I didn't meet his "criteria." Days later, he switched it up again: "How about dinner and a movie?" Two days following this invitation, he messaged me to say that he was looking for someone with "a more slender appearance and more natural hair color." These communications, although irritating, were also fascinating. His fluctuating tendencies revealed a core ambivalence, mood swings between anger and longing. With this last insult, the last message he had sent me, it seemed that my silence had hurt him, and he wanted to hurt me back.

I suppressed comebacks:

"At least you know what really matters in a relationship."

"I'm grateful you've finally realized that we aren't compatible."

"Please, go away—and stay there."

With these two Nice Guys, our face-to-face interactions went badly almost immediately. In other cases, our interactions soured after friendlier initial exchanges.

❧

One Saturday night, entirely on a whim, I met a man for drinks at a hotel bar. Talkative and enthusiastic, he seemed loud and fun. I wondered how much he'd already had to drink. When the bar closed, he told me he had a room upstairs and a bottle of wine he wanted to share, assuring me he'd be a perfect gentleman. After I declined this suspect invitation, we made dinner plans for later in the week. I half-jokingly told him I wanted to see what our interactions would be like when he was sober.

A day or so later, he texted me his phone number: "So you have my number for whenever you want it." I thanked him and asked for his last name. He told me. "Let the vetting begin . . . no criminal record. I really own a business ☺." I thanked him again.

"And yours????"

"Smith," I replied.

"Jennifer Smith? Well that won't be hard to narrow down ☺☺."

"I'm teasing you," I clarified.

"I see . . . ok . . . all in due time ☺" But I heard from him the very next day: "So I give you my name and number and you are quiet and don't reciprocate. Hmmm perhaps I should ask where things stand? Are we still on for tomorrow?"

"Hi." I replied. "You sound uneasy. I apologize. Yes, I'm still interested in getting together if you are."

"I'm fine just wanting to know why you would ask for my name and not give me yours."

"I didn't mean to upset you," I explained. "Because you offered your phone number, I thought it made sense to have your name to go with it. I've had a few bad experiences and don't usually give out my number and full name until I know someone more."

"I'm not upset . . . just curious."

Despite these words, he seemed quite wounded when we met for dinner. He was waiting at the restaurant, already having ordered a drink at the bar. He approached me, drink in hand, as I chatted with the hostess—a former student. When she asked if we needed a table, I turned to him, but he simply shrugged. After we were seated, he told me that I looked "beautiful as usual." This was nice. But then he launched into a diatribe. He talked, at length, about how unfair it felt for him to be "lumped in with assholes." He talked about how he was a Nice Guy, a trusting person. Why couldn't I see that? He showed a complete lack of self-awareness. His behavior demonstrated clearly why some women are cautious about sharing personal details. This man wasn't nearly as nice as he seemed to think he was.

Internally, I recoiled. Externally, though, I validated his feelings. I observed that he felt resentful, as if he was being treated unfairly. He agreed that this was true and added that he was a trusting person by nature, even though there are "lots of crazy women out there." The clear implication was that a good person is a trusting person, a person like him. He seemed to be saying that because I hadn't trusted him with personal information, I was lacking in an essential, desirable quality. I said that I was happy for him—glad that he could be trusting and that he'd never been made to feel unsafe while meeting strange women in public. Although he wondered aloud what might have happened to make me hesitant to share my full name, he quickly moved on to other topics. Apparently, he wasn't interested enough to ask.

During dinner, he showed intermittent moments of self-awareness but couldn't seem to change course. He'd speak at length, then complain that I didn't talk enough. He repeatedly said he felt like he was being interviewed. I apologized, asking what he'd like to know. When he posed a question, I'd answer it and ask the same of him. At that, he'd launch into a monologue and eventually follow up by saying, once again, that I wasn't talkative enough. This cycle repeated.

Eventually, he asked about my other dating experiences. Because of the resentment in his tone of voice, I asked if he really wanted to know about them. He said no, he didn't. Instead, he told me that he had expected this evening to be a waste of time. He also said that he wondered if I had really loved my husband because here I was: on a date. He aimed but missed. I responded, simply, "My husband wanted me to be happy. He loved me always—no matter what." After the server brought the check to our table, I offered to pay for dinner because he had bought our drinks earlier that week. He replied, "Oh, is that your exit strategy?" This was a man who struggled to give and receive generosity. I knew we'd not be seeing each other again.

⁊

One final Nice Guy deserves mention. Initially, he seemed smart and thoughtful. We had some common experiences; we both taught undergraduates and had Italian mothers. He seemed mild-mannered, with an "ah, shucks" energy. In fact, this particular Nice Guy told me that most women didn't tend to like him because he wasn't an alpha male. But it quickly became clear that his dating history included red flags. He was in his mid-fifties but tended to date emotionally troubled women who were at least twenty years younger.

Having learned to be more direct, I told him that I'd only be interested in being friends. For hours—literally, hours—we discussed his years spent dating much younger women. Based on his descriptions, these women wanted his money, his attention, and his support. They feared abandonment and rejected him first, before he could reject them. Many of these women seemed to have histories of trauma. The latest woman, age thirty-three, asked him for $2,000 so she could buy a new cell phone; her parents wouldn't front her the money. He said he'd found her a way to get a good deal from a specific store, but she wasn't interested. After he refused to give her cash, she stopped responding entirely. He pointed out that she had an infant and didn't seem to be using good financial judgment, although he "didn't want to act like her father or anything."

Based on our extensive conversations, I asked him why he seemed most drawn to much younger women with daddy issues. Why did he always focus on younger women?

His response: "I'm not telling you to fish in a pond you find uncomfortable, but age is not the same as maturity."

"Of course, it isn't," I replied, "but ghosting hardly seems like a mature move."

He agreed. I pressed on, pointing out that I'd been married to a man twelve years older than me and that I was now a widow. I suggested that there are reasons to consider pairing with people who are more similar in age.

He shot back: "No. But would you have given up the last twenty-five years with him to avoid being a widow now?"

I was stung. "We were together for almost nineteen years," I told him. "I can't do that kind of calculation." I commented that the first year after Tris's death had been incredibly difficult, and particularly milestones such as Valentine's Day.

Ignoring my last comment, he pressed on. "Okay, correct the number, but the question stands." Hot white rage pricked, momentary blinding me before I protested: "I hate that question. Is this pain worth it?! How can you ask that?"

He pressed on again. "Sorry. But isn't the pain your answer?" I regressed, reduced to wordlessness. Still, if I were to address him, here's what I'd say:

"Don't use my marriage to justify your predatory behavior with overly young women. Don't suggest that I'm somehow lucky to feel so raw, heartbroken, and exhausted. You say that you envy 'alpha men,' overt sexists who are so-called provocative and testosterone-driven. But you are implicitly sexist, which feels just as insidious."

※

If I could say anything to any of these Nice Guys, I'd take the conversation even further:

"You ignore what women like me tell you. You focus on what you want, not what we say. You fail to listen. You feel superior. You know best. You tell yourself you're a giving person who puts others first—a real good guy. Yet you make deliberate decisions to interact with specific women who act in ways that confirm your misogynistic beliefs about womanhood. And even with women who are less vulnerable, you pull for these same behaviors. Then you scratch your head, wondering why it's so hard to be a Nice Guy, stung by how unfair it is . . ."

That Nice Guys always finish last.

Love Letter Number Three

Dearest,

This morning, I went to the jewelry box to touch your wedding ring. Then I went into your closet and pulled out two random shirts. One has dark stains on the collar from a nosebleed. Apparently, I never laundered it. I hid these shirts in my own closet for safekeeping. At some point, although I don't know when, it'll be time to clean out your closet and dresser, to donate your shirts and suits. But not *these* shirts. These I'll keep forever.

I'm doing better, overall. The ache is less constant, less sharp. I still don't eat but sleep comes easier at night. My brain is more or less back online. Yesterday, I revised an academic paper. Sometimes I listen to books instead of sad music. On Monday night, Maddy and I argued about her upcoming report card. I was calm. I didn't cry. You were with me, helping me to stay grounded.

The sun is shining more often now.

I'm different, though: older, sadder, wiser. The pain is less intense, less visible, but it has altered me. There's a deep furrow between my eyebrows. I've shrunken and softened. Nowadays, people strain to hear my voice. Some changes are for the better. Daily, I try to be more like you: generous, wise, focused on what matters—the big picture. I try to keep perspective. I'm in less of a rush, less tied to rules and lists, less focused on being in control. Control is an illusion, after all. I try to think about humility, about humor. You had an abundance of these gifts.

Every day, there is joy and there is sorrow. I try to acknowledge and embrace all the feelings, without bitterness or cynicism or denial. I try to be open and giving, like you. I try to remember that everything, somehow, will work out. I try to see that, even when things don't really work out . . . well, that's just another version of things working themselves out.

As I'm shaped by grief into a newer version of myself, I wonder how you'd experience me now. Would you have liked a calmer, quieter wife? Someone more patient, more open, less judgmental? *Yes, of course. I'm sorry, my love.* Now that it's too late, I see the ways in which I could've done more and been more, when I was yours.

J

The First Second Date

My first second date, after becoming a widow, was with some-one I'll call "Sean." For the first several months, I stuck to first dates only. Yet when Sean and I had coffee together one afternoon, he seemed caring and fun. He seemed like someone I might enjoy getting to know.

For our second date, we met just before noon outside of a bowl-ing alley. I arrived early, having never before been to this location, worried about getting lost and being late. Once parked, I checked my phone and read a sweet message from a friend. Then I looked up, still grinning widely. Sean was there, also early, waiting, and grinning. I hugged him hello. He seemed pleased, though he hung back a bit.

We entered the alley. I received size seven red and black shoes. These were perfectly color-coordinated with my red, long-sleeved shirt and black jeans. I picked up a seven-pound ball, red-hued. This felt matching. It felt symmetrical. It felt good. But the air inside the bowling alley was cold, so chilly that I lost all of the feeling in my right foot. And I was nervous, feeling out of place. The last time I had bowled was over twenty years ago. I was about to humiliate myself in this brave new world of actual dating, but I didn't care!

Bowling was surprisingly fun, if awkward. I bowled badly, some-times wobbling, always unable to aim. *How appropriate.* Still, Sean was genuinely encouraging. We cheered each other on. I did make a few lucky shots. Sean was a much better player. He made several strikes and spares. Once, he made a split. We high-fived. He pointed at a small bird flying in the room. *How odd.* He pointed out that there seemed to be bowling etiquette: wait for the person in the next lane to bowl before approaching. *How observant.*

We played our first game, and my score was shameful: sixty-nine. I laughed. Of course, it was! *How humiliating.* His score was close to double mine. Unfazed, Sean offered options. We could take a break, grab a drink, get a snack, or play another game. Unsure, I declared, "Let's try again!" He observed that we seemed to have warmed up, that we were doing better. *Yes, we were.* He bought some water and insisted that I take the first sip. We began again.

In our second game, I had fewer lucky shots and earned a still humiliating (but less scatological) final score: sixty-one. Sean also scored lower the second time but still broke a hundred. We had talked more, focused less on the game. After he'd paid for our games and shoes, I asked him if I could buy him lunch. He agreed. We headed out, my car following his small gray hatchback.

At the restaurant, he ordered falafel. I invited him to try my favorite dish: savory shrimp. He liked the shrimp, although it was too hot at first. Later, he prompted me to eat before it was too cold to enjoy. We sought a comfortable temperature, the feeling of just-rightness.

He told me about his family, including the heartbreak of years of estrangement from his now teen daughter. He described how he reaches out, ever hopeful, ever patient. I was moved. He showed me a photo. She had his same gentle smile. He was facing his own form of grief, his own one-way relationship. He described trying to remain patient and open, engaged and sad, but not bitter.

Did I talk too much? Probably. I told him about some of my other dates, of enduring monologues, and of fielding intrusive questions. I told him about having a huge group of supportive friends, about how work has been a haven for me, about how right now I do more personal writing instead of my typical academic work, about how I'm both functional and sad.

Did I ask the right questions? Who knows? He told me his last name. He told me about his ex-wife, his counselor, his health, his frustrations at work, and his own dating experiences. He described talking to women who had then stopped talking to him, who had disappeared without a trace. He talked about meeting people who were entirely unrecognizable based on their earlier texts and phone calls. He expressed the hurt of receiving insensitive comments. One woman had told him that she didn't want to be involved with a man who had any ear or nose hair. "Like a mammal?" I retorted, indignant. Impulsively, I reached for his hand.

I said that I felt certain that I'd like to see him again but uncertain about what I may be ready for.

He stroked my fingers and touched my ring. He made me blush, stammer, smile, and laugh. He made me remember how easy it can be when two people just click; when there's connection, safety, and also, a spark. *I had forgotten that feeling.* I hadn't known if I'd ever feel it again.

Dessert

On our third date, Sean and I shared breakfast. We met at a coffee shop parking lot and then he drove us to a crowded local diner. I'd never been to this part of town before. I didn't recognize where we were going, or even how we arrived.

This diner is famous for pancakes the size of steering wheels, pebbled with fruit or chocolate chips or different types of candy. We sat across from one another at a large booth. He suggested, and I agreed, that we share two entrees: one savory, one sweet. We pondered the choices. There were too many options. He said he preferred meals over dessert, but the diner's dessert selections were irresistible. I wondered what I preferred these days. Once I would've said sweet. Now, it's not clear.

Also, I hadn't had any coffee yet. So, who could know?

The truth is this. Starting a few months after Tris died, I began to eat as little as possible. Instead, I drank coffee and then hot tea. Most days I didn't eat until dinner. When I started to feel dizzy, I'd grab some walnuts or almonds. I never ate breakfast. I absolutely never ate dessert. Dessert felt off-limits, unnecessary. It felt unfair to indulge. Food was for sustenance, not enjoyment or pleasure. There's an empty place, a place deep inside that was untouchable, unfillable. *Why even try? Food is love—and my love is gone.*

Unloved by Tris, I shrunk. I took up less space in the world. I dug through boxes of old clothes to find ones that fit. I had to buy new jeans and new bras. I craved the feeling of constriction around my neck, back, and waist. A family friend asked me how much weight I'd lost. A friend at work praised my sleeker look. Men began to gaze at me in a new way, maybe perceiving me as sexually available. As I contracted into myself, grief and emptiness consumed me. My outer form shifted. Ironically, these shifts unintentionally appealed to others.

In the booth, Sean said, "I have a sweet tooth—but I don't like when things are too sweet, like cake icing." I nodded. He pointed out the cannoli pancakes, "These are unbelievably good. Do you like cannoli?"

Well. That's quite the question. Do I? Cannoli is my favorite dessert. And it's a meaningful one. On our third date, Tris cooked us a three-course Italian dinner that included minestrone soup, chicken parmigiana, and homemade cannoli. It was delicious. I had teased him that he was cooking his way into my heart. That night, we had kissed for the first time. That night, he had told me that he wanted me to be his girlfriend—but he had a short life expectancy, and I deserved to be involved with someone healthy who could give me children. That night had changed everything for us.

Back at the diner, we ordered a Swiss and mushroom omelet and a cannoli pancake to split. My head full of memories, I wondered if I could swallow.

As we waited for our meals, we talked. Sean told me about his work history. He owned a business for ten years, then sold it to move north. He hoped to be closer to his brother, to make a better life for his daughter, and to salvage a difficult marriage. But their marital problems were surprisingly portable and sticky, not to be left behind. Sean worked different jobs—in a bank, in a grocery store—looking for contentment. On his path, he ended up seeing a therapist. One day, she asked, "Why not just move out?" This was a profound new possibility, one he had never before considered. And then, he did. That was a move that changed everything for him.

Our meals arrived just as I started to tell him that I had a confession to make. Sean responded with trepidation, "Uh oh." I switched course. Instead of confessing, I told him it felt like he was waiting for me to say something terrible, something catastrophic. He agreed. He described the disappointment of getting to know someone and, along the way, learning that they aren't going to be compatible. He admitted that he sometimes wonders if something good might be too good to be true. He admitted that he often waits for "the other shoe to drop."

I hesitated at this, wondering if I'm someone with too many shoes, ones I might drop onto him—bruising him, disappointing him. And then I charged ahead, admitting that I don't eat dessert anymore, not since Tris died. Sean's eyes widened in surprise. He asked why I hadn't told him that earlier; we could've ordered something different. I tried to explain that I wanted to try, wanted to be ready, wanted to take a new step. I told him I didn't want us to order anything different and hadn't told him on purpose, so that the order would stay just as it was. He took this in. Still, he seemed slightly unsettled.

He cut the omelet in half and moved the eggs and half of the pancake to his plate. I halved the rest of the omelet for myself. I began taking small bites of hot, cheesy egg. It felt daring. It was amazing. This tasted both familiar and unfamiliar. This tasted delicious. Sean encouraged me to try the pancake. I told him that I was working up to it. Eventually, I did. I halved the rest of the pancake before spooning it onto my plate. I began, as before, with a small bite. It felt daring. It was amazing. And it was painful. My eyes filled with tears. I kept gazing down, murmuring how good it was. It was so delicious.

Apparently, my pain was transparent. Sean expressed appreciation for me trying something new. He squeezed my hand. He told me that he had noticed that I don't eat much. He wondered if I was shy or if didn't want to eat much in front of him. I told him that, with him, I ate *more* than I usually did. It was the truth.

We didn't finish the pancake. The server brought us a box. "I can't have that in the house," Sean said. "If I have it, I'll eat it. I have no willpower." I nodded in recognition. That was also me, once—before I became hollow, a shell.

He drove us back to the parking lot where I'd left my car. We listened to music and talked for a while. He stroked my hair. It felt wonderful. I reached for his hand. I told him that I wondered if it would be better, more rational, to wait to see him again until I was more ready. What I didn't tell him was this: With him, I began to taste happiness. With him, I felt myself starting to shift, to open. I felt afraid and also courageous, vulnerable, and capable. I felt myself slowly becoming able to receive the sweetness still left in the world.

*

I stopped seeing Sean after a couple more dates. He became somewhat possessive and unhappy that I wasn't ready for any type of commitment. He said that he worried that I wanted to find someone more handsome, more educated, more like my late husband. I couldn't reassure him. Although we weren't compatible or looking for the same type of relationship, I'm grateful to Sean. Because of his kindness and his patience, I went on a second date and also ate dessert – two new steps forward.

Green Light

This is a story of a belated second date. I had met "Joe" for the first time several months earlier. In fact, he'd been my third date after I'd joined an online dating website. At the time, I'd still been raw and reeling from the very idea of being single after almost two decades. When we first met for coffee, Joe had been the more active conversationalist. I was withdrawn—still unaccustomed to small talk, still wildly distracted by disbelief and a strong sense of surrealism. *How did I get here?* How was it even possible that, after being happily married for almost two decades, I'm now single? Now on a date? What is a date, anyway? And what am I doing here?

After maybe twenty other dates, I better appreciated Joe. I admired his work accomplishments and his dedication to being a good father to two young daughters. During our interactions, he expressed optimistic, interesting ideas. He was formal, almost stiff, although he spontaneously hugged me after walking me to my car. Overall, he seemed sweet, and he seemed to like me. But I didn't hear from him again.

Late one weekend night, I was logged into the dating website answering messages. Idly, I scrolled down my inbox and saw that Joe was also logged in. Impulsively, I reached out: "Hi. I hope you're doing well!"

I don't know why I did this. Possibly, I was relaxed because of the wine I was enjoying. *Why not?* Possibly, I was just lonely. For many people who are widowed, nights and weekends are especially tough. There are few distractions during the lazy, unstructured days and nights—especially at night. Although I've always been a homebody, at night and on weekends, I found myself restless, on edge, habitually prone to leave the house. Often, I went to the gym to work out until it closed at 11:00 p.m. The previous Saturday evening, after someone had reached out on the dating website, I had met him for a drink just to have a place to go, a reason to leave our now-lonely house.

Joe wrote back. I felt rewarded for my impulsive move:

"Hi Jennifer. I'm okay, was just up watching some TV before bed. You're so nice to reach out! I think I dropped the ball (got busy with work and a bit weary of dating) and didn't respond after we met. It wasn't a decision, so much as not making one. I've honestly felt badly about not responding."

. . . and later:

"Would you like to meet to chat and catch up? My schedule's pretty flexible."

I said yes. We texted a few times after setting up our date, each expressing happy anticipation. Neither of us seemed to be playing it cool. I appreciated that he seemed enthusiastic and interested. He seemed thoughtful about my feelings and concerned about texting too late. More than that, he simply seemed glad to be in touch with me again. I felt the same way.

For our belated second date, we met for evening drinks. He walked in, smiling, just about a minute after I arrived. From the parking lot, he had happily texted me that he had driven straight to the restaurant without hitting a single red light. I laughed and suggested his luck could have metaphorical significance—a positive, cosmic sign. Perhaps inspired by Joe's positive encounters with green lights, I ordered a Green Lantern: Midori, coconut rum, and pineapple juice. He ordered a beer. We sipped our drinks slowly while talking for two full hours, unaware of the time passing.

Joe talked about multiple stressors at work. These included stress about restructuring a program and a colleague's failed promotion. I was struck by his dedication to doing a good job and his openness to change, despite the challenges change often brings. We discussed our shared distaste for ongoing political conflicts. We each appreciated general spirituality more than specific faith traditions. After I pointed out that politics and religion were often forbidden topics for a second date, he joked that we could talk about sex next time.

We also discussed lighter topics: entertainment, children, and pets. We found that we enjoyed watching some of the same TV shows with our daughters. We discussed our children's musical inclinations and feelings of restlessness during long concerts. We talked about our birthdays. I told him mine was in August and he jokingly asked if it was "the entire month." I laughed and agreed, yes, it would be a *looong* celebration.

I liked that he was a creative thinker who considered fantastic possibilities. He liked that I have good listening skills and attend to what others say. He asked me if I'd be considered "socially intelligent," and claimed that he wasn't. I objected. After many first dates, I could confidently praise him for being a good conversationalist and for being funny and thoughtful. He seemed to accept the compliment.

When the server brought our check, Joe asked if he could buy our drinks, saying that he felt indebted to me for sending him the message which reconnected us. He looked apologetic. He explained that, even though our first date had gone well, he'd felt ambivalent about seeing me again because my husband had passed away. He said he worried about me being a widow. This wasn't because I'd always love my husband, which he thought was wonderful, but because he worried that I might be hurt if things didn't work out. Internally, I appreciated that he'd recognized my raw vulnerability. Externally, I tried to reassure him that everything had worked out. Yes, I'd been very skittish when we first met—but now I felt on more solid ground, more confident in what I was doing. This was pure truth. Revealing it felt like pure happiness.

Joe looked impressed. He said he didn't always feel he knew what he was doing, but he hoped we could have a third date. I said that I hoped so, too.

He walked me to my car and hugged me. He wondered aloud whether, again, he'd hit all green lights on the way home. He also wondered what it would mean if he hit all red lights. We laughed. Later, he texted to say he'd had a "really fun time" and he wanted to see me as soon as possible. He seemed excited to see me again. Or maybe I was projecting my own feelings onto Joe, because I felt excited to see him again. Now—unlike before—I felt ready.

॰॰

Joe and I went on two more dates. Although everything seemed to go well, he abruptly stopped texting me. I don't know why. After I sent a final text and he didn't respond, we were no longer in touch.

A Full and Happy Life

My first kiss with a man who wasn't my husband took place during a happy afternoon after a morning full of grief.

Earlier that day, I had driven downtown to sign a new will. Although my appointment was scheduled for 8:00 a.m., I had arrived at 7:30 a.m. Standing in the hallway outside the locked door, I texted a friend about my newly combative relationship with time. Once he arrived, my lawyer was kind and efficient. Signing the will was a relief. It also was sad. I felt profoundly disoriented driving around the parking garage, looking for the exit, finding my way out into the world.

Slightly later, at 10:30 a.m., I attended the second meeting of a new grief group—the third one I'd joined. I teared up listening to others describe their pain, our pain, my pain. The sadness was heavy but also made lighter by sharing. We discussed the ABCs of grief (different mourning-related words: *alone, anxious, abandoned, awful*) up to the letter "i" (*isolated, insomnia, irritable, intense*). This week's activity was to write a letter to ourselves from our loved ones. I tried to access my inner self, the place where I carry Tris. I tuned into his voice, his wisdom, his love. Here's what I heard:

Beautiful Jenny,

I'm proud of you. You're taking care of everything all on your own. I knew you could do it, but I'm sorry you have to. Long ago, on our third date, I told you I'd die an early death. You didn't believe me. I couldn't make you understand. You're the great love of my life. That'll never change, no matter what happens. I trust that you'll have a full and happy life. I trust our children will have all they need. I trust you and believe in you. Trust yourself. You can do this, and know that I'm still here, always, forever.

Your Tris

I could clearly hear Tris's voice as my hand transcribed these words. While writing, I sobbed audibly, chest heaving. From around the room, sympathetic heads turned toward me. I was too sad to be embarrassed. The elderly man next to me patted my arm and recommended additional groups I might also join. I excused myself to escape to the restroom for a moment of solitude, reassuring the facilitator that I was intact—just needing the facilities. She trusted me. I stumbled haltingly down the hallway, alone.

After the group ended, I slowly drove home and gathered myself. And then I drove, for the first time, to the apartment of a man I had started dating.

It turned out that he lived in a huge, old, beautiful, purple building with rainbow flags flying. I parked next to his car in the lot behind the building but was confused about how to enter. *Which door should I open?* I wandered around to the front and entered into a foyer with a locked interior door. Still confused, I texted him. He descended the stairs and led the way.

We sat and talked. He held my hand and caressed my cheek. I thought about how dangerous this might be, going to a man's apartment alone. And I thought about how safe I felt.

At some point, I wanted him to kiss me. I told him so. He stood. His hands moved to my face, cupping my cheeks, and his face moved closer. Then his lips touched mine. It was such a gentle kiss. I was amazed. He shifted, kissing my cheek, my neck. I moaned. His lips returned to mine. My heart raced. My stomach leapt.

My mind struggled to make sense of this first kiss. *Is this really happening?* It felt surreal. I hadn't kissed another man in almost twenty years. Emotions flooded me: arousal, joy, pleasure, heat, surprise, affection, and longing. I realized that part of me had wondered whether it would be possible to have these types of feelings again with someone who wasn't my beloved husband. I also realized that some emotions were unexpectedly absent. I didn't feel sad. I didn't feel guilty.

I was grateful to feel safe. He was respectful, asking me to sit close to him. He was warm. I shivered, vulnerable yet bold. In some ways, he was the shy one. Maybe because it was more recent for him to suffer the sting of real romantic disappointment. Maybe because I had set clear boundaries; I didn't want to mislead him about what would *not* be happening. Maybe I seemed fierce. After all, I was bearing the unbearable and had learned that my spine is solid steel. Who knows? But, I did know this: I didn't cry. I wasn't sad. Instead, I felt full of hope for the full and happy life that I might still have, a different life than the one I had once enjoyed—but full and happy, nonetheless.

As my visit was ending, he offered to walk me to my car. He said that there was a shortcut, but the steps were steep. He offered to show me the way. I descended, feeling somewhat dizzy as I haltingly made my way down into the bright world.

Tenderness

Tris was a most tender soul. He'd carefully observe my facial expressions, body language, choice of words, and general mood. Sometimes he'd offer a direct observation, expressing concern or asking for more information. More often he was indirect, wordlessly acting to ease my mind, soothe my nerves, and soften my heart. He might stroke my cheek, rub my shoulders, or hold my hand. He might offer me warm toast layered with butter and cinnamon sugar.

Before Tris died, I had his comfort. I also had psychological defenses: feelings of safety and security. These invisible gifts once grounded me. My brain was shielded by a layer of protective denial with ideas like: "The world is predictable," and "Good choices lead to good outcomes." I took all of that for granted. Now, salty tidal waves of grief wash over me. My eyes and lungs fill, sting, burn, and overflow. There's no escape. At times, it feels as if I'm drowning from the inside. More than a year after his death, there are still mornings when I wake, alone in our bed, and there's a sharp pain in my chest. All I can do is breathe and wait. All I can do is hold on.

I'm both grateful and tearful when others see me—*really see me*— and respond with care and tenderness. Feeling moments of love, or even approximations of love, offers a sense of connection with the person in the moment, as well as with Tris. At these times, I can remember. At these times, I have a type of emotional access. It's a portal into the past. I feel what it felt like to experience tenderness with my beloved husband who was so full of comfort, so full of love.

I've been fortunate, in the aftermath of Tris's death, to be surrounded by care, by tenderness. Some care has been direct: "How are you? What can I do? You look tired. Are you getting enough rest?" Some care has been less direct: "I've brought you (soup/a book/a plant)." Family and friends have encircled and embraced me.

Even acquaintances show me love. On the day that would've been our nineteenth wedding anniversary, I booked a massage. After the therapist had kneaded my knotted shoulders, she left a gift: an anniversary card and a bouquet of fresh flowers. Later, I visited a psychic who read my tarot cards. She told me that I was touching other people's lives and that the love I send into the universe will return back to me. My future, she said, is full of happiness and connection, light and love.

I wait for this future, impatiently.

In this partly cloudy present, experiences of tenderness both soothe and sting. The sting is especially acute when men who never knew Tris act in similar ways. A date kissed me. He tenderly touched his lips to mine, gentle and firm, restrained and ardent. This first kiss of ours built and grew into a sweet crescendo, new and yet familiar. My heart sang as I cried all the way home, enjoying the pleasure of the present while also mourning the memory of Tris and his kisses. At these moments, my heart aches, even as I feel Tris gently nudge me toward the promise of tender connection.

Dating is supposed to be fun and light. I try. But often I'm unable to play the dating game. I break the rules. I'm an open book. At times, pain flashes across my face. At times, tears fill my eyes. At times, I can't make eye contact. In those moments, I reveal myself as lost and lonely, sad and self-critical. New people have no reason to care. Still, some do.

One afternoon a date texted me a question. I answered, "Monday

afternoon," but then revised: "No. Lie. 11:30 a.m. Almost afternoon."
He pointed out, "Lie was a strong word." I replied, "Yes. Agreed.
Not a great choice of words." He then wrote: "Be kinder to yourself,
Jenny ☺." Later, he texted: "Are you ok?" I pondered how unexpected
it felt for someone to see me—*really see me*—through a few phrases
and then to respond with compassion. This via text, when a nonre-
sponse would be so much easier. In a forum where many people disap-
pear completely, quickly ghosting one another with ease. (Tangential
point: "ghosting" is a terrible word, especially for the bereaved.)

I went to the theatre with a date. In the parking lot, as we walked
to the entrance, he reached for my hand. My heart leapt, thrilled to
feel this unexpected, everyday form of intimacy. We saw a musical
featuring flawed people feeling stuck, looking to connect even in
impossible circumstances, expressing pain and hope through poi-
gnant lyrics. The songs were beautiful. As the music swelled, this man
wrapped an arm around me. I leaned my head against his strong,
solid shoulder. In that moment, although I was grateful to be with
him, I missed Tris terribly.

I spoke with a date about my project of learning to relate to adults
as a single woman. I confessed that I'd had several new first dates
recently and jokingly called myself "a slutty widow." He strongly
objected, calling my choice of words "harsh" and "inaccurate." He
was eager to reassure me and express appreciation for my attempts
to try to embrace my new reality, to reconstruct a new life. Like Tris,
he focused on the positive, generously offering me the benefit of the
doubt without evidence or reason.

Once, before Tris died, I had teased him about having an open
marriage. At the time, I'd been reading *The Ethical Slut*, a classic book
about consensual polyamory. And at the time, this option had seemed
just as likely for us as moving to Mars—both of us shy, introverted,
apt to blush. But now I'm practicing polyamory, in a way, because
Tris is still here, still with me. The two of us are dating, together.

He whispers, "No," when I meet someone rude or entitled. He nods, "Yes," when I encounter generosity or feel pleasure. At the time that I had met Tris, when I was twenty-five years old, I'd never before been romantically involved with anyone with such tender inclinations. I'd never before met anyone so open, so generous, so unconditional. Now, even in death, he is my anchor, my compass, my heart.

Dating in middle age is different. There are wolves of all ages. Still, I've met multiple caring, tender-hearted men. As I take halting steps forward, as a single dating woman, there's reason for hope.

Moments of caring feel both wonderful and unspeakably sad. These moments are tender. They poke at my bruised heart like fingers picking at a half-formed scab, itchy and aching with the slow growth of healing. These moments remind me how it felt to be part of a great love. They remind me what it was like when someone wonderful had my back, was on my side, was devoted to me. These moments remind me that, once upon a time, I had tossed my fragile glass heart out to someone who did all he could to guard it, to treasure it. Once upon a time, someone wonderful was completely fulfilled by our shared life together.

To experience small moments of tenderness—to contemplate that such tenderness might be possible even without Tris in the world—hurts.

Dualities

I'm widowed. And I'm single. I'm stricken with grief. And I'm intensely involved with someone new.

The possible future without my beloved is chilling. The possible future with someone new is electric.

For almost twenty years—almost half of my life—wiry tendrils of affection, adoration, lust, and love were interwoven into my marriage. Now my beloved husband is dead. Amid the rubble of my new life, I've rediscovered these sharp bright feelings. They're partially unburied, tangled into a tight thorny knot. Loose strands dangle. *What will happen if I pull the red wire?*

I'm with someone new, someone different. He breathes me in. His touch is affectionate, arousing, adoring. The room feels cold. Still, I'm flooded with gratifying sensations: heat, heft, happiness. The smell of his skin, the taste of his lips, the feel of his hands; all overwhelm me with exquisite pleasure. At the same time, just below the surface, there's also an exquisite sadness.

My lips and my heart feel scorched, new, raw, and bright pink. Grief has burned me alive.

I'm passive, surrendering to a growing urgency. Carefully, gently, he removes my jeans, my bra. *Yes, yes, please, God, yes.* I want to moan. *I can't believe this is happening.* And, just as strongly: *no, no, no!* I want to cry. *I can't believe that this is happening.* Torn, I remain wordless. Although I'm silent, my body speaks. I writhe. Shivers bloom across my shoulders and upper arms. My neck arches. My breath catches. My spine elongates. My toes curl.

This new person is tender and attentive. He makes me feel attractive, desirable, and safe. He takes me in, exploring the architecture of my body and how it responds. He observes my shiver as he traces his fingers across my lower right hip. He hears my gasp as his lips graze the back of my neck. Pleased with these discoveries, he repeats these movements . . . over and over. Attraction ignites desire, which builds into a full scorching flame. I melt and dissolve, helpless in pleasure that feels both familiar and entirely new.

I'm overcome by tremendous gratitude to be with someone so generous and patient. I'm also overcome by a profound heartache that rises from under the surface, ignited by the joy, commingling the past and the present. Again, he breathes me in. I'm falling, suspended, with him and yet—also alone. Exposed and yet—also hidden. I find myself wracked with sobs. He wraps his strong arms around me. This man who embraces me is tender and caring. His tenderness releases within me a deep, visceral longing for my tender, caring husband who is gone. *Forever.* I weep.

REFLECTING ON HOPE

- How have you coped with the loneliness of loss? How have your perceptions of yourself been affected? How do other people perceive you? How have their perceptions of you changed since your loss?

- The author wrote, "There's no competition among meaningful relationships." In what ways do you agree with this statement? In what ways do you disagree?

- How do you manage interactions with people who make assumptions about what you need or how you should behave? When, if ever, do you find people treating you in hostile or condescending ways? When and why do people make negative judgments about a grieving person who builds new relationships?

- Your loved one played particular roles in your life. Do other people fill in for any of these roles? What does that feel like? When and how does having someone else take on those roles affect how much you miss your loved one?

- How did your relationship with your loved one affect how you relate to new people you meet—people who never had the chance to meet your loved one?

- In your experience, what does it mean to "move forward" after a loss?

CONCLUSION
All You Need

One morning, yoga class was unusually focused on compassionate self-acceptance. After some gentle and mindful movement, we spent most of an hour flat on our backs, inhaling and exhaling, slowly and deeply. Paradoxically, our work was rest. We worked to quiet our bodies and minds, to let go, to release our physical energy and our mental expectations. The teacher opened class with a suggestion: We have all that we need within ourselves.

All you need is already in there.

This was a startling idea. *Could that be true?* Along with hope, I felt a deep sadness build and peak.

The teacher continued. Sometimes we get cloudy and we lose sight of what is within us. In the same way, on a day with clouds or fog, our view of the sun is blocked. Although we've lost sight of the sun, our perception doesn't change reality. *The sun is there.* Even while hidden from view, the sun still warms us, providing energy and light. We can remind ourselves that, even if today it's out of sight, at some point we'll see the sun again.

Weather patterns are also created, internally, by our busy nervous systems. There are storms of swirling thoughts. Tidal waves of emotions build, crest, and crash. In yoga, we move and stretch, straining to attain perfect posture and accurate alignment. Ironically, instead of clearing our minds through movement, in yoga we may make judgments about how flexible, how strong we are. These judgments can cloud our vision. We fail to notice that, on our mats and also in our lives, we are already perfect. We are all and have all that we need to be.

In my brain, the teacher's words crystallized into a simple phrase: *I am enough.*

As a perfectionist, this feels like a radical idea. It feels especially radical given my situation, as someone grieving a beloved spouse. Our pairing is now halved. Alone, I'm so much less than we once were together.

Grieving feels like doing, not being. It's grueling, taxing work. I've stumbled to regain stable footing after the world collapsed. The strain has been physical, mental, emotional, and spiritual. I've been trying (so, so hard) to manage, to mourn. I've been trying to rebuild, to be practical and yet also open to the universe, to the unknown. I've tried to connect to my beloved in whatever ways might still be possible—looking for signs, for meaning, for love. It's taken tremendous effort to start to adapt to my new life. It's taken tremendous effort to embrace all of the tasks my husband once took care of: domestic, financial, familial. The strain is tangible. Others can see it, feel it. Possibly they can smell the tangy, acidic desperation. I'm now a single mom. I'm now a sole homeowner. And I now represent him to others: our children, relatives, neighbors, coworkers. There's so much responsibility, so much to do. Plus, I make every mistake.

Along with these new obligations and roles, because I'm grieving, I move like someone in a dream pushing hard to advance even slightly forward. There's also mental fog. I'm cloudy, not clear. *Really, is there still a sun?*

Stumbling and cloudy, I judge myself. I also feel myself judged by others about how flexible and strong I am not. How do I even do this? What's the right way to be a Good Widow?

The yoga teacher said we are each already whole and perfect, just as we are. And yet, without my beloved, there's a huge hole in my heart. *Can I be whole and also be missing a part?* She said there's no need to struggle against what is. There's nothing to be gained by fighting against truth. And yet, without my beloved, there's a huge hole in my life. *Can I accept the unacceptable?* These are some of the paradoxes of grief.

Later, reflecting on the class and my emotional inner tsunami, I detect a small, still voice. From deep within, for many, many months, this small voice has been asking: *if I'm very, very good—if I try very, very hard—please, oh please, can this all be over?*

And in a way, it's like the yoga teacher somehow heard. *I'm sorry, no. This. Just. Is.*

That was the bad news. But she also offered this: We can accept thoughts as ideas, which may or may not need to be considered. We can embrace emotions as signifying internal shifts. Emotions are always transient, possibly important, possibly not. We can accept our bodies, our postures, and our lives. Just as they are. Just as we are. We can breathe and be. Nothing has to be done, gained, practiced, or developed.

Maybe so. If I can accept that Tris, although gone, is also a permanent part of me, maybe I also can believe: *all I need is already here.*

AFTERWORD

Last night, Tris came to me in a dream. This was unexpected. He hasn't been in any of my dreams for well over a year. The dream felt happy. But after waking, I cried.

In the dream, it was daytime. Sunlight poured in from the windows on the first floor of our house. Many adults and children were walking around, talking, busy. Maybe we were all headed out for a picnic? Two green Tupperware containers were stacked neatly on the counter.

As I stood near the kitchen in the foyer of the house, Tris came into the kitchen. He strode purposefully past me and began to head up the stairs. Shocked and thrilled, I called out, "Wait! Come back!"

He turned, offering his shy, sweet smile. "Oh, yes, of course. Hello." He hugged me. It was wonderful to feel his arms, his love. My heart filled.

And then he told me that he had to go; he had things to do. He was composed and caring, levelheaded and loving. He was himself.

He said goodbye and headed upstairs.

ACKNOWLEDGMENTS

After Tris's sudden death, my family was surrounded by love. Countless individuals deserve thanks for all they did to support us during the darkest hours. These include relatives, friends, neighbors, colleagues, and former or current students. You know who you are. I love you all.

Beth, Bruce, Ellen, Jenn, Karen, Laura, Lisa, Mary, Paula, Silvia, and Tacianna: You read my early drafts and encouraged me to keep writing despite overwhelming sadness, fear, and shame. You're all my tribe, my family, for always. Clea, Deena, Hillary, Jim, Maria, Mary, Michael, Sarah, Tori, and Tracy: You *know*. Thank you for sharing with me and for letting me share with you.

Claire and Theo: You were the most loving, effective, amazing grief counselors a widow could ask for. There are no words. Aimee, Kyle, LeeAnn, and Susan: You teach yoga and so much more. Your wisdom and compassion have helped me to heal and have given me hope. Christine: You pored over each line of each essay; thank you, thank you for helping me clearly communicate my story. Alice and Maddy: You're both clear-eyed and generous; thanks for all of your proofreading help.

Maddy, Jonah, and Hana—you're my whole heart.

ABOUT THE AUTHOR

Jennifer Katz was born and raised in South Florida along with a twin brother, a younger sister, and a toy poodle named Muffin. At age twenty-five, she earned her degree in clinical psychology and met Tristram Smith at a job interview. After she was hired, they became friends . . . and then more. Jenny and Tris married and moved to upstate New York with a son. Widowed at age forty-five, Jenny now lives with her teen daughter. She loves yoga, musical theater, and broccoli. She's an award-winning professor who teaches about gender, sexuality, and helping relationships. This is her first book.

SELECTED TITLES FROM SHE WRITES PRESS

She Writes Press is an independent publishing company founded to serve women writers everywhere. Visit us at www.shewritespress.com.

Splitting the Difference: A Heart-Shaped Memoir by Tré Miller-Rodríguez $19.95, 978-1-938314-20-9

When 34-year-old Tré Miller-Rodríguez's husband dies suddenly from a heart attack, her grief sends her on an unexpected journey that culminates in a reunion with the biological daughter she gave up at 18.

Naked Mountain: A Memoir by Marcia Mabee. $16.95, 978-1-63152-097-6

A compelling memoir of one woman's journey of natural world discovery, tragedy, and the enduring bonds of marriage, set against the backdrop of a stunning mountaintop in rural Virginia.

Filling Her Shoes: Memoir of an Inherited Family by Betsy Graziani Fasbinder $16.95, 978-1-63152-198-0

A "sweet-bitter" story of how, with tenderness as their guide, a family formed in the wake of loss and learned that joy and grief can be entwined cohabitants in our lives.

The Art of Losing it: A Memoir of Grief and Addiction by Rosemary Keevil $16.95, 978-1-63152-777-7

When her husband dies of cancer and her brother dies of AIDS in the same year, Rosemary is left to raise her two young daughters on her own and plunged into a hurricane of grief—a hurricane from which she seeks refuge in drugs and alcohol.

Broken Whole: A Memoir by Jane Binns. $16.95, 978-1-63152-433-2

At the age of thirty-five, desperate to salvage a self that has been suffocating for years, Jane Binns leaves her husband of twelve years. She has no plan or intention but to leave, however—and there begin the misadventures lying in wait for her.